TI

THE LOWLAND CLEARANCES

Scotland's Silent Revolution, 1760–1830

Peter Aitchison and Andrew Cassell

This edition published in 2019 by
Birlinn Origin, an imprint of
Birlinn Limited
West Newington House
10 Newington Road
Edinburgh EH9 1QS

www.birlinn.co.uk

First published in 2003 by Tuckwell Press Ltd, East Linton

ISBN 978 1 912476 85 5

British-Library Cataloguing-in-Publication Data
A catalogue record for this book is available from the British Library

Typeset by Hewer Text (UK) Ltd, Edinburgh
Printed and bound by Clays Ltd, Elcograf S.p.A.

Contents

Acknowledgements

This book is based on the research conducted in preparation for a series of programmes transmitted in May and June 2003 on BBC Radio Scotland. We are grateful to Maggie Cunningham, the head of Radio Scotland, for not just allowing us permission to proceed with the book, but for embracing the idea that led to *The Lowland Clearances* project. As a Gael she appreciated from the outset the importance of setting the record straight on what actually happened to the majority of the Scottish population who lived below the Highland Line. We are also indebted to Jane Fowler, commissioning editor and head of features, for her support and criticism and to Kate Hook who supervised the budget and somehow managed to keep us organised. Thanks are also due to other members of staff at the BBC, especially David Neville who co-ordinated and produced the drama sequences which have inspired some of the elements of this work; and to Michael Calder who was the sound engineer on the radio series. When we were comfortable in a warm car or at the table of a restaurant, he was still tramping about the countryside trying to obtain the right 'noises' to ensure that the programmes were of the highest technical quality possible. Mic was also a key part of the production team. His input was substantial and invaluable.

Of course producing documentaries and writing books requires time which is not always a ready commodity in the life of a busy newsroom. But our colleagues, Blair Jenkins, Stewart Easton and Phil Taylor, made it possible for us to meet our commitments by an indulgent and generous organisation of work rotas. For their patience we would also like to thank Colin Blane, Sean McGrath and John Morrison whose constructive criticism was a source of constant inspiration.

Much of what follows was derived from interview transcripts and we are indebted to all of those academics and individuals who agreed to take part. Professor Tom Devine of Aberdeen University in particular was generous with his encouragement and advice. Tom has done so much to make Scottish history accessible. He has a unique power of oratory and an almost messianic zeal for his discipline. We never tired of listening to him outline events that took place centuries ago, yet to which Tom seemed able to give a contemporary feel.

From that starting point we tapped into what is a remarkable seam of historical debate. All of our interviewees provided fresh and moving perspectives on a contentious subject. Professor Chris Whatley of Dundee University opened up the dynamic area of social, economic and political protest, whilst Professor Callum Brown of Strathclyde University provided the religious context to a turbulent age. The Historiographer Royal, Professor Christopher Smout, was more sanguine on the outcome for the majority of lowlanders and his wry and comprehensive overview gave us much to ponder as we drove around Scotland. No story of lowland clearance could be attempted without acknowledging the appalling events that later occurred in the Highlands. Dr James Hunter provided that reference point and a lot more besides. The long discussions we held with Dr Hunter, in the warmth of his kitchen and the chill of the hillside overlooking Kiltarlity, provided a tangible link between north and south. Scotland is fortunate to have such a wealth of academic expertise in these matters and they will all recognise their influence in this work.

A sense of empathy with the past existences of ordinary people was delivered by Sandy Fenton at the National Museums of Scotland and by Gavin Sprott who took us to the Museum of Scottish Country Life near East Kilbride. There we were given a vivid appreciation of the hardships of daily life in pre-Improvement times. Gavin, who as well as being a renowned ethnologist is also one of Scotland's leading authorities on Robert Burns, then gave context to some of the work of our national bard. In Burns' cottage in Alloway he explained how the family were almost brought to ruin by the great changes. But for the income from the Edinburgh edition, they might well have been forced to emigrate.

Millions did leave Scotland in search of a new life, which led us to the door of two specialists in this field: John Beech who unearthed a treasure-trove of original documentation and Dr Marjory Harper of Aberdeen University whose recent work shows that the exodus was far from being highland-dominated.

History without a human face can be interesting – but history which provides the real stories of real people can, we believe, be much more illuminating. We found the true testimony of cleared lowlanders on the Scarborough Bluffs, an outcrop overlooking the shores of Lake Ontario in modern-day Toronto. A few taps on the modern tool of the internet had brought us the story of James McCowan, exiled in the 1830s when he lost his hold on land in Lanarkshire. It was to those bluffs he brought his family and it was on that escarpment that we met with his descendant Bruce McCowan. Bruce and his wife Bea gave us a marvellous welcome and then opened our eyes to the reality of what life had been like for the McCowans through a huge array of original source material that they had spent years amassing.

Back in Scotland we found more evidence of lowland settlement at the deserted fermtoun of Lour in Peeblesshire. Through the trained eye of amateur archaeologist Ed Archer incongruous hillocks were transformed into what they had once been – the base of a few scattered cottages that were thrown down when the laird decreed the people should move. Whilst in the Borders we saw the other side of the story of improvement through the archives of John Home Robertson MSP. His ancestors prospered from the changes, and he welcomed our interest because, he said, whilst a lot is known of what happened to those who did well, history is largely silent on what happened to those who did not.

The story of the Galloway Rising, when hundreds of ordinary peasants, outraged and distressed by attempts to enclose their land, took to arms, is well documented. But local historian Alistair Livingstone brought the episode to life through his dramatic commentary at the very site of the rising. We are grateful to Alistair and to all of those who have given so generously of their time and expertise and who have answered our questions with patience and good humour.

Our thanks are also due to the staff and librarians at a number of institutions: the Mitchell Library and the Byres Road Library in Glasgow, the National Archives of Scotland and National Library of Scotland in Edinburgh, Helensburgh Library and Lochwinnoch Community Museum.

John and Val Tuckwell of Tuckwell Press goaded us onwards with a deadline that would put many news editors to shame. Like all deadlines, it concentrated our minds, but also meant long evenings and absent weekends from our families. A final, but heartfelt, thanks to our wives and children for their support, encouragement and perhaps above all else understanding.

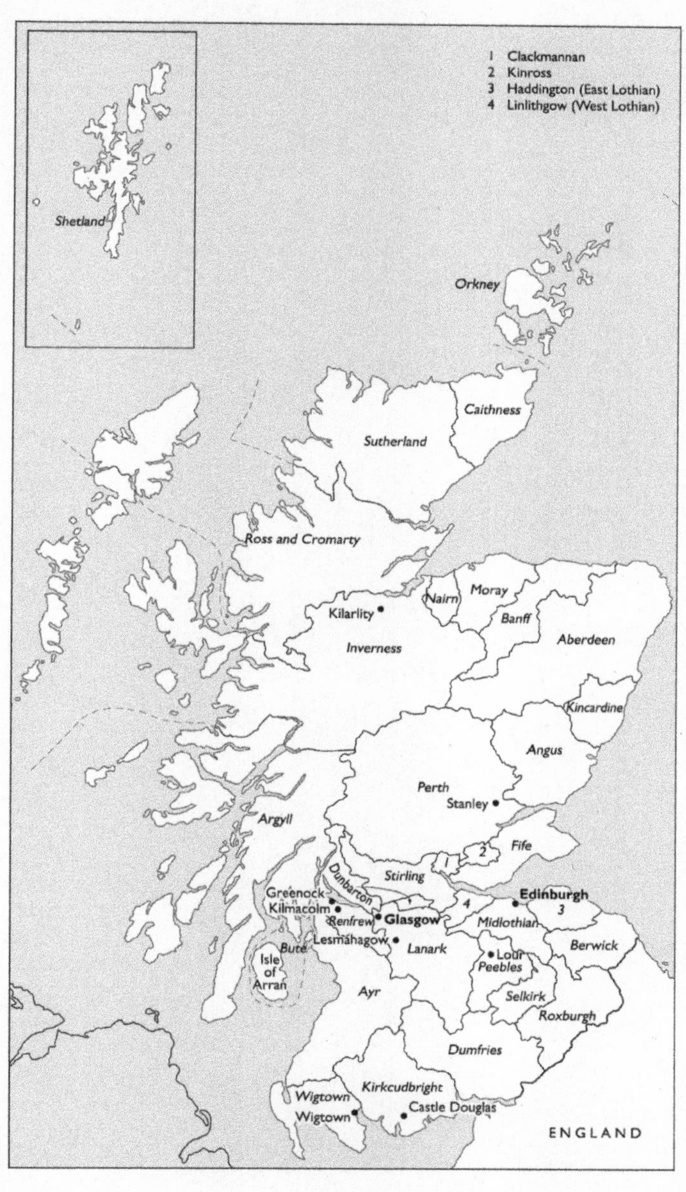
1 Clackmannan
2 Kinross
3 Haddington (East Lothian)
4 Linlithgow (West Lothian)
Shetland
Orkney
Caithness
Sutherland
Ross and Cromarty
Nairn
Moray
Banff
Aberdeen
Kilarlity
Inverness
Kincardine
Angus
Perth
Stanley
Argyll
Fife
Stirling
Dunbarton
Greenock
Kilmacolm
Renfrew
Glasgow
Edinburgh
Midlothian
Lesmahagow
Lanark
Bute
Isle of Arran
Lour
Peebles
Berwick
Selkirk
Roxburgh
Ayr
Dumfries
Kirkcudbright
Wigtown
Wigtown
Castle Douglas
ENGLAND

CHAPTER ONE

Introduction

> 'The social dislocation in the rural Lowlands in the later eighteenth century has virtually been overlooked and though the Highlands have stimulated a veritable scholarly industry the Lowland Clearances still await their historian.'
>
> Professor Tom Devine, *The Scottish Nation*

Tom Devine achieved many things in his seminal and wonderfully readable account *The Scottish Nation* but for us as journalists and broadcasters it was this hanging question which intrigued. Like many Scots we felt we had a decent appreciation of the Highland Clearances, a raw sore on the national psyche which still has the power to shame; a despicable episode in our nation's past which destroyed a traditional way of life, which set clansmen against chieftain and sent a whole people overseas in the stinking holds of emigrant ships. It was a process predicated on profit and carried out all too often by the Sassenach factors of estates which once were clan-held, but now were claimed by the chiefs themselves.

In spite of recent revisionism, the reality and brutality of what happened in the straths and glens of the Highlands and Islands in the nineteenth century cannot be denied.

Yet here was arguably Scotland's foremost living historian almost casually introducing a whole new dimension to the story: The *Lowland* Clearances. As a phrase it has shock-value. Few outside academia have ever considered why it is that Scotland south of the Highland Line was *improved* whilst those who lived to the north and west of that imaginary divide were *cleared*. The more we considered the issue, the more nonsensical that use of language seemed. As we drove from Galloway, through the hilly uplands of Lanarkshire to the Trossach moorlands and on to the forests of Inverness-shire, what did we see? Sparsely populated territory, the ruins of long deserted steadings, and cud-chewing beasts. Large chunks of Lowland Scotland were mirroring the traditional picture of the deserted Highlands: sheep and cattle in abundance; people at a premium.

This book is not an academic work in the traditional sense. It has no footnotes and only a select bibliography. But as journalists we have spent a great deal of time teasing out the salient facts, and analysing the various points of contention from many of the nation's leading historians as well as amateur enthusiasts in both Scotland and Canada. What has emerged is a remarkable consensus.

The Highland Clearances did not just suddenly happen, and were not the result of planned ethnic cleansing by Lowland or English demons. There were many reasons why clan chiefs turned their backs on centuries of tradition. But perhaps the overriding motivator was the template provided by events in the south, which had taken place decades earlier. These events were known at the time, and have been referred to by historians since, as 'The Age of Improvement'. What actually took place from Berwickshire to Buchan, from Solway to Shetland, from Orkney to Aberdeenshire and all points in between was a wholesale revolution in agriculture. Over the course of two generations, or from around 1760 to 1830, the very structures of Lowland society were ripped apart; thousands of people were forced from their lands; hundreds of tiny settlements were abandoned or destroyed; an entire social stratum was eradicated and Scotland changed forever. These Lowland Clearances paved the way for the events which would later sweep through Highland Scotland. They were part and parcel of the same process. They ought to be called The Scottish Clearances.

Moreover it became clear that a by-product of the great changes which struck Scotland, north and south, was the creation of two countries. At the start of the eighteenth century there was no lowland-highland divide. Scotland was a peasant society, with one of the most backward agricultural systems in Europe. It was an almost wholly rural country, with Edinburgh at forty thousand and Glasgow at less than fifteen thousand people the only sizeable towns. Though the crops grown might have differed, and the land occupied was of varying quality, cottars in the Lowlands and clansmen in the Highlands worked the same runrig system of subsistence farming. They herded their beasts in the same way. They used the same implements. They occupied the same houses. A *butt and ben*, for example, was a Lowland term and a Lowland invention, adapted by the Highlander. Nor did language differences stand in the way of communication. English was by no means a standard for all. If some Scottish peasants spoke Gaelic, then Doric was the tongue of others, or Gallowayan the leid of others still. When they mixed or mingled, for instance at cattle droves, folk managed to make themselves understood. This was one Scotland.

Come forward to the nineteenth century and that homogeneity had fractured. Farming in the Lowlands was now about profit and production for the market. The link between people and the land had, for the most part, been broken. New 'planned' villages housed the surplus labour which had been forced out when collectivisation replaced the strip system. Some of these places seem incongruous to the modern mind.

Towns and then great cities gorged on the overflow from the rural Lowlands. Scotland experienced the fastest urban growth in Western Europe in the last two decades of the eighteenth and first two decades of the nineteenth century. Where one in ten of the population had lived in towns in 1700, the number by 1821 was one in three. Ranch-style estates replaced the patchwork of individual holdings, producing huge quantities of food and pulling in dramatically increased rents for the lairds who claimed legal ownership over areas of formerly common land.

The early nineteenth-century Lowland landscape looked very different from that of the Highlands and Islands. Lowland society, once almost as clannish, was now structured along the lines of class and wealth. These profound changes were achieved within the space of seventy years. Breakneck speed considering that so little had altered in the previous five centuries. And it had all happened peacefully, with no major unrest and no social upheaval. Or did it?

There is now general agreement amongst historians that what took place between 1760 and 1830 could, with some accuracy, be called a Lowland Clearance. There can be no disputing the documentary evidence on the wholesale movement off the land of people whose families had lived there for generations. As well as estate papers, court records and individual accounts there is also the happy historical accident of Scotland being one of the best-mapped countries in the world.

Dutchman Jan Blaeu produced forty-seven detailed maps of Scotland in 1654, based on the earlier work of Timothy Pont. In every Lowland county there were literally dozens of settlements, known as fermtouns. Each contained a number of families, averaging perhaps fifty to a hundred individuals. They lived and worked together, farming the runrig strips of the infield, and herding their animals on the outfield and the common land. These fermtouns were the rock of Lowland stability. Some, like Lour in Peeblesshire, could trace their history back to the Iron Age or even earlier. The cottars of Lour had endured Roman occupation, and successive invasion and liberation during the long wars of Scottish Independence. They had lived through famine and plague but they could not survive the whim of a new landowner who, in the mid-eighteenth century, decided to rationalise his estate. The people were replaced by sheep and the village disappeared, only to be rediscovered by archaeologists two centuries later.

Fermtouns across the Lowlands suffered the same fate as Lour. Nineteenth-century maps contrast sharply with those produced by Pont and Blaeu. Regular fields with the occasional village dotted on the landscape were now the norm. If fermtouns survive at all, it is usually only by accident. Individual farms, those created from the aggrandisement of several family holdings, sometimes kept the name of the original settlement. But the people for the most part have gone.

Another remarkable resource, which confirms the impact of agricultural improvement in mid- to late eighteenth-century Scotland, is the twenty-one volume Old Statistical Account of Scotland. Compiled by Sir John Sinclair in the 1790s, this was a digest of returns, usually from Kirk ministers, from virtually every parish in the land. Some gave more information than others on population, agricultural practices, industry, topography and suchlike. But in Lowland parish after Lowland parish commentators noted, sometimes in the most powerful language, the full impact of what was going on in the countryside. Ministers reflected on the increased productivity of the estates and also on the often baneful effects on the local populace. Cottages were pulled down, villages deserted, whole areas made devoid of people especially in marginal upland parishes. It is a picture which equates almost perfectly with that of the crofting townships of the nineteenth-century Highlands and Islands.

Those who remained on the land now paid many times more rent than previous tenants, and the lowest elements of rural society – the subtenants and cottars – were fast disappearing. It was the cottars who moved, or were moved, into the new villages which were being constructed at the edges of the big farms, or who were drawn to the burgeoning industrial towns and cities of Scotland's central belt – or who went overseas in a wave of lowland migration.

How were the Lowland Clearances achieved? What were the factors which led the lairds to drastically change what had been unaltered for so long? What impact did these changes have? Was it, as Tom Devine believes, 'a silent revolution'? Or were there significant protests which brought Scotland to the brink of bloody upheaval? Could the changes have been avoided? What sort of Scotland might we now have but for the Age of Improvement but which could just as accurately be called the Age of Clearance? And why do we know so much of what happened in the Highlands yet so little of what took place in the Lowlands?

These were some of the questions we sought to answer in the BBC radio documentaries. The same questions we asked of people who have worked extensively on the period. The answers they gave, and the evidence we gathered, form the basis of this book.

Professor Devine was perhaps being disingenuous in his plea for a historian to come forward and tackle the subject. Along with his team he has spent many years researching and analysing the structure and nature of Lowland society using reams of documents and estate records. Devine's motivation, beyond the need to seek out truth, was to remedy that imbalance between the cottage industry of Highland history and the relative neglect of the rest of Scotland where seventy to eighty per cent of the population live. He expected to find protest. Perhaps he even hoped to find some significant event or movement which shouted out against the changes. Beyond routine vandalism and petty crime, however, Professor Devine's studies revealed a remarkable quiescence in the face of tremendous upheaval. Even though an entire social layer – the cottars – who made up a third of the population in some parishes vanished during the Lowland Clearances, still, he says, there was no threat to the established order.

One of the reasons for that, says Devine, is the speed of change. Although the Clearances happened in a relatively short period of time, they were piecemeal and haphazard. There was no overall sense of nationwide change until that process was all but complete. Professor Devine also says that many of the evictions were carried out within the legal framework. Starting from the later seventeenth century, leases began to be written down, and when these expired tenants were obliged to leave, thereby allowing multiple farms to be amalgamated into a more productive and lucrative single unit. This 'clearance by stealth' had the cloak of legality and was backed up by the still considerable feudal power of the local laird or lord. The landowners also used the fig-leaf of legislation passed in the 1690s to justify their appropriation of huge areas of common land. In Berwickshire, for example, the Homes of Wedderburn owned only 1000 acres, yet in the 1750s and 1760s they were able to seize a large portion of the north of the county which they proceeded to 'improve'. There is no doubt that the productivity of this part of the eastern border, the Merse, leapt as a consequence. But there is also no doubt that this action pushed people out of rural life – people who depended on access to the common land and who lived on the edge of subsistence.

For those forced from the land there were choices – sometimes unpalatable, but choices nonetheless. Cottars could become linen-weavers in places like Coldingham or fishermen in the booming coastal centre of Eyemouth. Many of the landowners who were in the vanguard of introducing new farming methods, men like John Cockburn of Ormiston in East Lothian, also built villages to house the displaced labour. Others followed suit in a wave of construction. Professor Christopher Smout has identified around a hundred and thirty of these communities. Although they were a uniquely Scottish solution to the problem of what to do with surplus labour, Smout is clear that there was no altruism involved. These were little more than holding centres for people who were needed in the still labour-intensive harvest season. During the rest of the year they were put to work in mills or factories, the profits of which generally went to the laird. All the while they continued to pay rent on their houses to the estate.

It would be wrong to infer that the clearances were all about 'push'. In both the Lowlands and in the Highlands there were significant 'pull' factors which drew people away from the land. While this may have been underplayed when explaining the depopulation of the Highlands, it could well have been overplayed in traditional accounts of the Lowland improvements.

It is not difficult to appreciate the attraction of towns to those used to the unrelenting harshness of scraping a living from the soil. This process of movement developed its own momentum as friends and relatives sent news back to the countryside of how their new lives compared. For some the urban swap was but a stepping stone to emigration, and new research from Dr Marjory Harper and John Beech has revealed the true extent of what was a massive shift of lowland Scots. As Dr Harper reveals, more attention is paid to highland migration to Canada and elsewhere because it came suddenly. But lowland emigration was just as significant and it is now evident that far more people left the Lowlands than ever departed the Gaelic-speaking areas of Scotland known as the Gaeltachd.

One such family was the McCowans. They had been tenant farmers in Ayrshire before they were forced to move in the first wave of clearances in the West of Scotland. For a while they managed to attain the lease on a small coal mine and got a foothold on the land at Stockbriggs, near Lesmahagow in

Lanarkshire. But the family were bankrupted again when a new owner raised the rents and, despairing of a future in Scotland, they opted for the adventure and danger of a new life in Canada. It was either that or the slums of Glasgow. Within fifteen years of arriving penniless on the shores of Lake Ontario, the McCowans managed to acquire 800 acres of arable land on what is now regarded as millionaires' row in downtown Toronto. Bruce McCowan, descendent of the original settler, has traced not just his family tree but has also amassed a huge collection of papers which confirm the fate of one victim of the Lowland Clearances. The McCowans' story is one which must have been repeated thousands of times over. They, like the other emigrant families in Toronto, rejoice in their lowland legacy: the Weirs, Purdies, Scotts and Davidsons. These were all Lanarkshire folk who left Scotland at the same time and settled in Canada in the same area.

Here is yet more evidence that emigration to Canada, Australia and New Zealand was not simply that of the Highlander. In the main the Highlander was in the minority.

The idea of a Lowland Clearance and the suggestion that without these events there could have been no similar exodus of people in the Highlands may seem a controversial conclusion. Yet it was one which Dr Jim Hunter, author of the acclaimed book *The Making of the Crofting Community* felt comfortable to endorse. He, like other academics, was uneasy about the use of blanket terms such as 'improvement' and 'clearance'. As Dr Hunter pointed out, lowland Scotland extended from the English border to his own home at Kiltarlity in Inverness-shire, and included the Northern Isles. Large parts of what many regard as the Highlands are actually within the orbit of lowland agriculture.

The Highland landowners, clan chiefs in the main, chose a different route to maximise their income. But when crofting and kelping failed, from the start of the second decade of the nineteenth century, they looked to do as their southern peers had done. They looked to 'improve' their lands. The topography of much of the North and West was ill-suited to crop rearing, and people were removed to make way for livestock, especially sheep. Something very similar had happened in the upland regions of Lanarkshire, Galloway and the Borders. The difference in the Highlands was the lack of any opportunities for the people who were deprived of their land. There was no industry to speak of, and though planned fishing villages were built along the coast, they could not provide for or sustain the population which was so suddenly, and at times violently, evicted.

Because the men involved in carrying through the Highland Clearances were often lowland farmers, the myth of a highland-lowland divide was created and cemented. The most notorious actor in this drama was Patrick Sellar, factor to the Duke of Sutherland. His infamous destruction of the crofting townships in Strathnaver is often quoted as an extreme example of the brutality of the Clearances. Less well known are Sellar's origins. His own grandfather was evicted from Morayshire in the earlier Lowland Clearances. In spite of his belief that the Highlanders were racially inferior, Sellar evidently thought that, like his own family, his victims would ultimately profit from what he saw as modernisation and progress.

There is some debate over whether Lowlanders, by the time of the Clearances, had already lost the almost mystical attachment to land which Highlanders still held. However, ethnologist Dr Gavin Sprott from the National Museums of Scotland believes that it's folly to dismiss the notion that Lowlanders had no natural affinity with the soil. Until the great changes of the later eighteenth century the land and what it produced was all that ninety-five per cent of the Scottish population knew.

As the whole issue of clearance or improvement has opened up, a growing number of historians are beginning to question just how acquiescent the Lowlands really were when faced with the upheaval involved. Professor Chris Whatley of Dundee University is clear that Scotland was 'on fire' with meal riots in the later eighteenth century and that these were rooted in the social dislocation caused by the displacement of communities. When people were thrown into the growing towns or mill villages they became wage slaves. But this proletariat still harked back if not to a golden age of plenty, then at least to a time when they were masters of their own destiny. They may have experienced dearth and occasional famine when on the land but there was a certainty about their existence. There were no such certainties in the new environment of profit and loss ledgers – when something called 'economics' led to unfathomable trade cycles which, in turn, could cause the mills to close. No work meant no bread – all the more galling to these erstwhile cottars when they saw their former homelands producing more grain than ever before.

Whatley also identifies the lessons the lairds learned from the only genuinely violent reaction to improvement. In the 1720s landowners in Galloway corralled their estates behind stone dykes, removing the people and bringing in cattle for sale in the lucrative English market. Local historian Alastair Livingston has done extensive research on the popular protests this evoked, culminating in a stand-off on the slopes of Keltonhill near Castle Douglas. The experience of the Galloway revolt was a chastening one. But did it affect the actions of the lairds elsewhere and much later in the century?

Other writers have suggested that protest may have been articulated in a fashion which we might find hard to understand today. Instead of placards and slogans, Professor Callum Brown believes the disaffected of the eighteenth century used the language of religion to make their points. He has examined schisms within the Kirk and charted the progress of disputes in individual parishes, which sometimes led to violent affray in church. Patronage rows, where the people defied the landowner's right to place his nominee in a pulpit, moved from south to north, as if following the spreading agricultural changes. This, to Professor Brown, was no accident. Religious dissent and the breakdown of deference to the lairds was evidence of a 'psalm-infested revolution'.

The nuances differ, the interpretations are slanted, but an historical consensus is clear. A process engulfed Scotland from around the middle of the eighteenth until the end of the nineteenth century. The first part of this period was dominated by the so-called Age of Improvement in the Lowlands, whilst the latter is characterised by the clearances of the Highlands. Yet the drive behind both was essentially the same. The population of Scotland began to increase sharply from the 1760s. Food supplies came under pressure, triggering agricultural innovation. At the same time peace with England and access to overseas markets further stimulated Scottish farming. These changes were successful in the Lowlands and created a settled and productive system which made the once ridiculed rural economy of Scotland the envy of Europe. When attempts were made to replicate that system in the Highlands, the result was very different. Arable land was less abundant, prompting many chiefs to put their faith and their money in sheep and cattle; people became superfluous.

This, then, is the story of how Scotland became what Scotland is today. We do not dispute the reality of the Highland Clearances nor do we seek to minimise the trauma they caused. Rather we wish to emphasise the historical continuum which led to those events and to give voice to those Lowland peasants who suffered just as badly, whose world was also turned upside down and whose lives were just as much changed forever when they were told to leave their lands.

CHAPTER TWO

Scotland before Improvement

> 'The ambition of the people at that time was not to improve the soil, but to reform the church; not to destroy weeds and brambles; but to root out heresy; not to break up the stubborn soil but to tread down the whore of Babylon, and the Man of Sin. Their attachment to every bad habit, and aversion to every improvement in agriculture were strong and deep rooted. In agriculture, as in other sciences, ignorance is the mother of devotion.'
>
> William Aiton, *General View of the Agriculture of the County of Ayr*, 1811

Today we live in a rapidly changing world. Change is part and parcel of everyday life; industries come and go, fashions and tastes are transient and endless building and construction projects seem to transform our street corners overnight. For those who lived and worked in Scotland before the Agricultural Revolution, however, this was not the case. At the start of the eighteenth century the way of life for the overwhelming majority of Scots had barely changed in centuries – a fact all too readily forgotten or ignored by the architects of the 'Age of Improvement' who scarcely concealed their contempt for those who stood in the way of progress.

Scotland in the seventeenth century was a rural world populated by about a million people locked into one of the most backward farming systems in Europe. Only a minority actually owned land but virtually everyone lived on it, worked on it and depended on it for survival. Most rented land from the laird and lived in small settlements, clusters of houses containing between five and twenty or so families. In the Lowlands these settlements were known as fermtouns and they littered the countryside. They formed the fabric of Scotland's rural farming community, a peasant society engaged in a communal system of subsistence farming.

There were a few towns but they were tiny by today's standards – amounting to no more than two or three hundred people – and they prospered as a result of being granted the privilege of trading rights. These Royal Burghs, places like Anstruther in Fife, were permitted to trade overseas, to import and export goods and to hold markets for local goods and produce. As commercial pressures grew in the first half of the eighteenth century other market centres were created, the burghs of barony, and some of these have grown and survive to this day – Paisley began life as a burgh of barony.

Commerce, however, was something which rarely troubled most Scots farmers of this period. They were too busy simply trying to produce enough food for themselves, with any surplus going to the landowner as rent. Cash payments for a lease on the land were modest. Instead a tenant was required to pay the rent in kind. This meant that on top of providing certain labour services a tenant would have to turn over a proportion of what he produced to the laird – often it was oats or bere, a type of barley, but it could also be poultry or cheese and milk.

An insight into the kind of obligations required of a tenant-farmer can be found in the Board of Agriculture Report on the County of Ayr 1793 written by Colonel William Fullarton:

> One half of the crop went to the landlord; and the other remained with the tenant, to maintain his family and to cultivate his farm. The tenants were harassed with a multitude of vexatious servitudes; such as, ploughing and leading for the landlord, working his hay, and other

> operations; which, from the nature of them, unavoidably interfered with the attention necessary on the tenant's own farm.

This rent-in-kind would have to be delivered to the landowner's granary or to a local merchant if the estate was close to a town or port. But, as Professor Tom Devine makes clear in his book *The Transformation of Rural Scotland*, the prices, delivery and transport arrangements were negotiated by estate factors – it was they, not the tenants, who dealt with the local traders.

The traditional method of farming in Scotland hadn't changed for centuries. Land was rented out to a single tenant or to a number of tenants who shared a lease. In general the size of these holdings was small, often not much bigger than twenty or thirty acres. They consisted of an infield area, which was worked continuously to grow crops and received the lion's share of manure and fertiliser, and a much larger, less productive outfield area where cattle were allowed to forage for grazing. They supplied the manure for the infield but were also often corralled to fertilise parts of the outfield ready for the planting of crops. Depending on where you lived, the infield was the 'croft land', the 'muckit land', the 'beirfay' or 'fey land'. Different crops were grown in different parts of the country and some areas were more readily suited to the rearing of livestock but everywhere the basic methods were the same and the infield was at its heart – the principal source of food and surplus for the rent.

The infield land lay closest to the turf-covered dwellings of the tenants, and the strips of ploughed, arable land were divided up and allocated to the various families. This was the system of runrig, known in some areas as rundale, which was the template for farming throughout pre-improvement Scotland.

In many cases the rigs of one family would be scattered from one fermtoun to another, and to reach each arable plot a tenant would have to use the various grass tracks which connected homes and fields. These were the loans or loanings which formed the main thoroughfares for humans and beasts alike.

All around the cultivated land were waste moorland, peat-bogs and huge plains of scrub and broom. These were regarded as common land and, though apparently barren, they made a vital contribution to fermtoun life. They provided rough grazing for livestock and turf for roofing and fuel.

To the modern farmer's eye it may all seem a confusing and haphazard way of cultivating the land. But by intermingling the rigs or parcels of land a community could ensure that each family received a fair share of the best soil, and that helped underpin the social stability and economic security of the fermtoun. This communal approach to farming also meant that tools could be shared, and it provided the one commodity that everyone needed: a ready supply of labour to help with the backbreaking and stamina-sapping work which the soil demanded if it was to yield its harvest.

But it was a primitive form of agriculture vulnerable to climate and disease. Crop yields were low and survival, especially in poor years, marginal. In the lean times many tenants were unable to meet the terms of their leases, forcing landowners to grant reductions, or abatements, in rent.

In February 1698 the teenage laird of the Carnwath Estate in Lanarkshire, George Lockhart, wrote to Sir James Scougall of Whitehill, one of his guardians:

> My tenants have sent me an address representing their sad condition, caused by a particular blasting and mildew which has wasted their crop as well as their neighbours'. Besides this, the crop of 1696 was generally bad

> throughout the kingdom. They have had this address attested by many of the ministers of Lanarkshire and Biggar Presbyteries, and they crave an abatement of that year's rent, as has been granted by other masters to their tenants who did not suffer as much . . .
>
> I realise the truth of their complaint and that the state of my tenants is such that without an abatement most of them will not be able to continue their holdings, and so will embezzle everything they can lay their hands on which should go towards the payment of their rent, for they will be without any hope of ever getting it all paid off. Whereby I shall be a far greater loser than I would be if I gave them sufficient abatement to encourage them to set to work again with some hope that they'll be able to live under me on their holdings. Besides it may be that the law would allow them more than I propose to give them. Therefore I desire the consent of your Lordship and of Mr Montgomery [Lockhart's other guardian] to grant my tenants an abatement of half their rent for the year 1696, as others have done before me, seeing it's against all equity that when the ground fails to produce its increase some consideration should not be given to those who work it. When they have got this abatement they will still be losers, but all their losses can be made up.

Often rent abatements still could not avert failure and that could have serious consequences for tenants. Those who didn't succeed simply went to the wall. They were forced to give up farming. Losing their hold on the land also meant the loss of rank and position in society. Such unfortunates would often end up as farm servants earning a poor wage from those who were making a go of things.

Clearly this was not a rural idyll – life was a hand-to-mouth existence in a vast countryside which was still largely uncultivated; a wild and forbidding place in which to try to eke out a living. Forget the settled rural landscape we see today with its solitary farmhouse set amid ordered fields, tree-lined lanes and neat hedgerows. The Scotland of the pre-improvement era was a place of open countryside with few borders or frontiers; where islands of cultivation struggled to survive amid the untamed and hostile landscape which surrounded them.

Even allowing for any improving sympathies he may have harboured, the Reverend John Mitchell in *Memories of Ayrshire* in 1780 paints a particularly startling picture of the rural landscape before the agricultural changes swept through the county:

> The face of the country was far from being cultivated or inviting. On the contrary, it appeared rough and dark, consisting greatly of heath, moss, patches of struggling wood and rudely cultivated grounds. The roads, made entirely by statute labour, were not smooth, irregular in their line, and far from being level in their track. The ditches which bounded them were seldom cleared out, and the hedges with which they were skirted being allowed to shoot forth into all their wild luxuriance were seldom cut and never pruned or clipped. Young trees were rarely planted, except perhaps in the hedge-row, in short the work of rural improvement had not yet begun, the country presented upon the whole a bleak and somewhat repulsive appearance.

To travellers from England, where the runrig system had long been abandoned, the Scottish system was primitive and wasteful. John Ray observed:

> The men seemed to be very lazy, and may be frequently observed to plow in their cloaks They have neither good bread, cheese, or drink. They cannot make them, nor will

> they learn. Their butter is very indifferent, and one would wonder how they could contrive to make it so bad. They use much pottage made of coal-wort, which they call keal, sometimes broth of decorticated barley. The ordinary country houses are pitiful cots, built of stone, and covered with turves, having in them but one room, many of them no chimneys, the windows very small holes, and not glazed.

Haphazard the landscape may have been, but Scottish society was well ordered, a system of rank and privilege colourfully portrayed in Robert Burns' poem 'The Twa Dogs'. This was a country where everyone knew their place and at the top of the pile were the governing elite, almost all of whom owned land.

Land was the key to power, political influence and personal authority. Feudalism died out in the Lowlands in the second half of the seventeenth century but until then – and for much longer in the Highlands – the families who owned land owned the people on it. In a martial society the more land you owned, the bigger the army you could raise.

It is not without justification that the current laird of Wedderburn, the Labour politician John Home-Robertson, describes his ancestors as warlords. His family have been landowners in the eastern borders of Scotland since the Middle Ages. More recently the area they owned was known as Berwickshire but in those days it was known as the East March and the Homes dominated everyday life, wielding immense power over everybody who lived there.

'Force of arms in those days was how many people you could call on to come and back you up,' says Mr Home-Robertson. 'The Homes either had the fear of the people or the loyalty of the people – and sometimes that might be interchangeable – but when the warden of the East March was called on by his King to call up his feudal levies to go to

Flodden, or wherever it was, they did that. That was what the power of the laird was based on.'

It was the landed class, those at the pinnacle of Scottish society, who were to drive through the changes traditionally characterised as the agricultural improvements. It was they who were to provide the momentum for the creation of large commercial farms and the clearances of people needed to make way for them.

As Chris Smout, Scotland's Historiographer Royal, noted, the landowner had all the cards in his hands: 'The landowners in Scotland were probably the most powerful in the whole of Euope. You find more restraints from landowners either by custom or by law than in France before the revolution and of course Britain never had a French Revolution, so they go on having these great powers. It was very difficult to resist the legal force of the landowner. Therefore people did not expect you could resist that force, and when eviction orders were served there was a tendency to accept them'.

The lairds of the old Scotland may have owned most of the land but they rarely worked it themselves. That was left to their tenants. The tenant class was small, accounting for up to a third of the rural populace, but it was a broad church. It included relatively wealthy farmers employing many workers and poorer families struggling to scratch a living from marginal hill country. Others were townspeople: professionals like surgeons, merchants or innkeepers who didn't live on the farms but took rent from sub-tenants who in turn might sub-let part of the land still further. Whether principal tenants or sub-tenants, farmdwellers or absentee, all enjoyed a considerable measure of legal protection. Even if their leases were only verbal agreements, when it came to removals they would still have to be given due notice and the correct legal procedures followed.

For the vast majority of rural people, however, the law

offered no protection. These were the cottars whose families would receive very small patches of land from tenants or sub-tenants in return for service. The cottars were the backbone of the countryside who did much of the menial but vital work. They rounded up the livestock, carried goods and produce from one place to another and were a pool of labour for the tenant to call on to make good his own service obligations to the laird. Some cottars were also skilled in the trades – they were weavers, carpenters or blacksmiths but they all depended on their smallholdings for survival. For cottars the work was hard when you could get it, and in the winter months working opportunities were limited. Most lived on the edge of poverty.

According to Gavin Sprott it was the cottars who had it really hard in the old-style countryside: 'Their situation was desperate if they failed because they fell out into this sump of not just unemployment in the modern sense; it was simply nothing. There was no means of livelihood, because there was no public expenditure worth speaking of. There were no unemployment schemes except the rather brutal one of the colliers.

'If you fell out of the system as a cottar life was absolutely grim and to us unimaginable. We think unemployment is bad. Life then for someone who had fallen out of the system would have been just indescribably grim because there was nothing to do and nowhere to go. People would harry you from one place to another. You would just have to beg, you would scrounge, you would live off the land, often through strong-armed tactics.' Such wretches were, in the parlance of the age, known as 'sturdy beggars' and contemporary literature is replete with references to the social ills attributed to them.

For all the toil and struggle which made up their life the poet Robert Burns, himself of farming stock, saw in the cottars a nobility few others in Scottish society would have conferred upon them. His poem 'The Cottar's Saturday Night' is a vibrant snapshot of the Scottish countryside and relates the scene as a cottar family spend an evening together preparing for the Sabbath:

November chill blaws loud wi' angry sugh;
The short'ning winter-day is near a close;
The miry beast retreating frae the pleugh;
The black'ning trains o' craws to their repose:
The toil-worn cottar frae his labour goes,
This night his weekly moil is at an end,
Collects his spades, his mattocks, and his hoes,
Hoping the morn in ease and rest to spend,
And weary, o'er the moor, his course does hameward
bend.

The poem affectionately describes a people who are penniless and who have few prospects in life. They'll never be rich nor even comfortably off and yet, says Burns, these people have a social grace and dignity which belies their lowly status:

From scenes like these, old Scotia's grandeur springs,
That makes her lov'd at home, rever'd abroad:
Princes and lords are but the breath of kings,
'An honest man's the noblest work of God;'
And certes, in fair virtue's heavenly road,
The cottage leaves the palace far behind;
What is a lordling's pomp? A cumbrous load,
Disguising oft the wretch of human kind,
Studied in arts of hell, in wickedness refin'd!

O Scotia! My dear, my native soil!
For whom my warmest wish to Heaven is sent,
Long may thy hardy sons of rustic toil
Be blest with health, and peace, and sweet content!

And O! may Heaven their simple lives prevent
From luxury's contagion, weak and vile!
Then howe'er crowns and coronets be rent,
A virtuous populace may rise the while,
And stand a wall of fire around their much-lov'd isle.

This notion of the dignity of labour and the working man, an idea expanded upon elsewhere in Burns's work, would have found little sympathy amongst the lairds of the time.

To the casual observer the cottars, who in many regions made up two-thirds of the rural population, would have seemed little different in manner or demeanour to many sub-tenants or poorer tenants. But there was a crucial difference. Under the old order the cottars had no legal right to hold land nor any legal protection if they were told to go. When the Clearances came, it was the cottars who bore the brunt of the improving zeal of the landlords.

One of the interesting features of the changes which were to engulf Scotland, it seemed to us, was the creation of two countries – the Highland Scotland of the north and the Lowland Scotland of the south. By the time the Clearances in the Highlands and Islands were in full swing in the nineteenth century there was an increasingly prevalent notion in Lowland society that theirs was a superior culture to that of the Gael, an attitude which seemed to help excuse what was being done in the name of Improvement.

For evidence of this you don't have to look beyond one of the central characters in the removals in the North: Patrick Sellar. 'He was utterly and totally contemptuous about the language and the culture and everything else about the people he was evicting,' says Highland historian Dr Jim Hunter. 'He felt the Highlanders were utterly benighted savages whose Gaelic language was just a badge of their backwardness.'

And yet prior to the Agricultural Revolution and the earlier clearances in the Lowlands this would have seemed ridiculous. Before the beginning of the eighteenth century Scots, both north and south, had much in common. They shared a communal approach to farming; the clansmen in the Highlands, like the tenants and cottars of the Lowlands, worked the same runrig system of farming. The crops they grew were often different and the cultivation methods adapted to take account of the varying quality of the soil, but they herded their livestock in the same way and the tools they used were similar. When James Small produced his new, more efficient plough, it was quickly adapted for use in the North. Contrary to popular belief there was an extraordinary amount of contact between Highlander and Lowlander. As Professor Sandy Fenton of the European Ethnological Research Centre at the National Museums of Scotland observes: 'By looking at the tools of agriculture you can see the process in fact'.

English was not universally spoken either, yet farmers from Ayrshire were still able to make themselves understood to those who might have the Doric of the North-East. So in spite of a language barrier life didn't stop at the Highland Line; there were trading links, and an increasing number of Highlanders sought seasonal work on the big southern farms or as fishermen on the east-coast herring boats during the summer.

One of the most obvious features which revealed this connection between Highlander and Lowlander was the very houses they built to live in. The 'butt and ben' style of accommodation was a Lowland invention which migrated north. This from William Aiton's observations in the *Agricultural Report of the County of Ayr* in 1811:

> About fifty years ago, the farm houses in the county of Ayr were despicable hovels; many of them were built in part, and some altogether of turf, or of mud plastered on stakes and basket work . . . That part of the building

> which served the family for lodging, sleeping, cookery, dairy etc denominated the in-seat, was about 12 or at most 14 feet square, with the fire either in the centre or in the gable On larger farms, another apartment, of nearly the same dimensions, and which entered through the in-seat, was called the spense . . . The other part of the building was occupied by the cattle, which generally entered by the same door with the family; the one turning to the trans-door by the kitchen, and through it to the spense, and the other turning the contrary way by the heck door to the byre or stable. The trans and heck doors were in the centre of the partitions, so that the people in the in-seat saw butt to the byre, and the inhabitants of the byre and stable could look ben to the in-seat; hence, houses built on that construction were said to consist of a butt and ben.

As standards improved, canopy-style fireplaces likewise moved north from the Lowlands.

One difference between Highland farmers and their Lowland counterparts, often quoted, was the way they regarded their relationship with the land; that the former somehow felt more connected to the land. Here we found some measure of debate.

What seems clear is that certainly by the latter part of the eighteenth century the relationship between the Lowland tenant and his laird was an economic one: there was an expectation that a lease, even at the end of nineteen years, might not be extended or renewed. In other words there was no belief that the land they farmed was theirs by right or that the landowner held it in trust for the people.

In the North and West, however, the clan system and martial attitudes endured. Here land was exchanged not just for rent but also for service. Tenancies continued to be granted, at least in part, on the basis of family connection and loyalty to the clan chief. Even after the Jacobite rebellion of 1745 and the events at Culloden, when the clan system came under sustained attack from the Hanoverian state, Highland landlords raised regiments for the British army by promising land in return for military service. During the French Wars recruitment rocketed. On the Isle of Skye, for example, nearly a quarter of the male population joined up – an island's sons exchanged for the promise of land.

'One of the reasons why there is so much emotion generated by the clearances [in the Highlands] is that there wasn't simply an economic connection [between tenant and landlord],' says Professor Devine. 'There was a renewal of the ancient Gaelic tradition of 'dulchas', which means in return for rental the landowner had an obligation to protect the people. When that was violated by clearance you can imagine the psychological consequences. But that's far removed from the world of the rural lowlands. Because by the time we are talking about, the second half of the eighteenth and early nineteenth century, the pattern there was a nexus of economic relationships, with very limited expectations of paternalism either from the local farmer or the local landowner.'

Even so there remained in the Lowlands a close relationship between land and people which had been unchanged for centuries, and Gavin Sprott feels that connection is often underplayed. He describes the idea that the Highlander was somehow more mystically connected to the land as romantic nonsense. Lowlanders, he argues, especially in pre-Improvement times, were totally dependent on it for their livelihood and survival.

Dr Hunter, whose book *The Making of the Crofting Community* chronicles the brutality of the Clearances in the Highlands, also doubts the notion that Lowlanders had any less affinity for the soil. 'There would have been a very similar affection for land and place and locality,' he says. 'By the eighteenth and nineteenth centuries people were making strong distinctions between the sort of society and even almost racial background of Lowlanders and Highlanders. But Scotland back into the Middle Ages was a society that was organised in much the same way and had much the same culture, whether Lowland or Highland. I think that these people [Lowlanders] felt much the same way about the place that they were attached to as Highlanders did. I don't think the experience of Highlanders – the sense of loss of leaving their glen – would have been all that different from the sense of an eighteenth-century peasant in the Lothians or wherever moving from his place.'

If, by the seventeenth and early eighteenth centuries, Lowland society was well ordered, that did not mean it was inert: more and more estate owners were coming to regard their lands as a source of income rather than as the basis of personal authority and power. The Scottish and English Crowns had been united in 1603 and formal political union with the 'Auld Enemy' in 1707 meant an end to the upheavals of war. But the peace dividend brought new cost pressures for the governing class. The landowning 'warlords' of old were now the new aristocracy who needed to be able to mix with and compete with the wider political elite based in London. They were spending more on the trappings of wealth – furniture, clothing and paintings – and they were travelling more, too. In the absence of war, fortified dwellings were rapidly being replaced by grander, more expensive, homes more suited to a man of means in an era of peace and commerce.

Throughout this period there was also a trend amongst landowners to place their relationship with their tenants on a more businesslike footing. Verbal leasing agreements, or tacks, were gradually replaced by longer, written rental documents and there was a steady erosion of multiple leasing arrangements in favour of single tenancies. The former tended to reinforce subsistence farming while a single tenant, where a farm was worked by one family and their servants, could ignore the traditions of the fermtoun and the communal restrictions and conventions they embodied. The single tenant was, at least in theory, free to try to maximise production to produce a surplus for the market.

But these, according to Professor Devine, were changes *within* rather than *of* the system. What was to follow in the decades up to 1760, however, changed Scottish lowland society far more fundamentally.

The old fermtoun communities, based on communal living and subsistence farming, existed in a world where commercial activity was increasing. The populations of towns like Edinburgh and Glasgow were growing, and small marketing centres, the burghs of barony, were being created to make the most of the trade in cattle and sheep between Scotland and England and in grain with the Scandinavian countries.

Against this background landlords abandoned the practice of asking for their rents to be paid in kind but demanded money instead. They also continued to phase out multiple leases with the result that more and more land was being rented out to fewer and fewer farmers. What this meant was that by 1760 the tenant class in Scotland was far smaller than it was at the start of the century, and those who remained as tenant farmers had a more business-oriented relationship with their laird. Their economic survival was also far more dependent on the markets and trade beyond the immediate confines of their farm.

However important these developments – and painful for those who were removed from their land – they were achieved through the landlord's manipulation of the lease system. Since leases were based broadly on a nineteen-year cycle, it was a long process. It was also patchy and piecemeal. It isn't difficult to imagine that in areas where markets were rapidly expanding – the border areas with England and those close to urban centres like Edinburgh – the pace of change was much faster than in remoter parts: the changes were evolutionary rather than sudden and cataclysmic.

In spite of these changes, however, and with the exception of a few progressive landlords such as Cockburn of Ormiston and Grant of Monymusk, the old farming techniques and cultivation methods endured – the landscape still bore the traditional runrigs of cultivation scattered on the infield and outfield areas of the farm.

But beneath this appearance of stability, the certainties of the old order had quietly ebbed away. Over the course of the next two generations the onset of capitalism and the rigours of the free market would ambush the countryside like a ferocious winter storm, wrenching many from the land and obliterating a way of life which had existed for centuries.

CHAPTER THREE

The Galloway Levellers

> 'Few movements were more foolish, more hopeless, and at the same time more eminently Scottish and sympathetic than this. It was the up-rising of the helpless Many against the strong Few, and, though defeated and well-nigh forgotten, it contains the root of the matter of many a modern and world-wide problem.'
>
> S.R.Crockett, *Raiderland*

It didn't look much at first: just a weather-beaten lump of rock, lodged in the middle of a stone wall, with an indistinct inscription carved into its surface. But as we tried to make out the figures and initials which seemed to be formed, our excitement grew – this was a moment of real discovery.

In the course of recording material for our BBC series on the Lowland Clearances we had agreed to meet local historian Alistair Livingston beside a wall which runs along the Old Military Road on the edge of the National Trust for Scotland's Threave Gardens near Castle Douglas. We cannot be certain – and enquiries are continuing – but it appeared we had stumbled upon a long-forgotten relic which confirmed an extraordinary episode during a tumultuous year of rebellion by the tenants and cottars of the South-West of Scotland.

In 1724 Galloway was convulsed by revolt. Bands of men and women were travelling around the area tearing down the stone walls or dykes erected by the landowners. The wall which runs along the edge of Threave Gardens, next to Keltonhill, is said to be the only one which was left standing in the whole of the Stewartry of Kirkcudbrightshire. The stone we had identified appeared to confirm local accounts, handed down through generations, that some of the so-called Levellers had left their mark to commemorate the event.

So how was it that this apparently unremarkable, moss-covered wall – now barely more than a few hundred metres long – came to be preserved?

That depends on which of two accounts you believe. According to one version the Levellers, or 'Rabblers' as they were sometimes termed, were met at Furbarliggat, at the foot of Keltonhill, by the local minister the Reverend William Falconer. Here by the power of his oratory he is said to have persuaded the group to desist from their wicked ways and leave the dyke standing.

There is, however, a more colourful version preserved in the stories emanating from contemporary eye-witnesses of the rebellion. This account holds that the laird of the estate, Captain Robert Johnstone, accompanied the minister to meet the band of levellers. Both men addressed the crowd, informing them that the wall had not been erected to divide up the estate but merely to shield the laird's land from the public road. No tenant or cottar family had been evicted and Captain Johnstone promised that every person on his land would continue to have and to hold his house, his yard or garden, and the usual quantity of corn sown. It seems their eloquence went down well with the crowd. But what may have helped further were the barrels of ale and the bread and cheese provided by Captain Johnstone: the beer was drunk, the dyke spared and the laird, apparently, cheered for his kindness.

It is a diverting, even vaguely amusing, tale. But the event at Keltonhill was an isolated and all-too-rare outbreak of conciliation during a period blighted by bitter confrontation and violence.

Not that the South-West of Scotland, and Galloway in

particular, was any stranger to the violence and turbulence of upheaval: few areas of the land suffered more during the religious struggles of the seventeenth century.

When the Stuart King Charles II was restored to the throne in 1660, he also restored himself as the ultimate authority in ecclesiastical matters and revived the authority of the bishops in the Scottish Church. This was heresy to Scottish Presbyterians, and many ministers, known as Covenanters, left or were forced to leave their parishes, preferring instead to hold alternative open-air services to the gatherings at the official Kirk. These meetings were outlawed as treason and troops were despatched to enforce the King's will. The result was the doomed Covenanters' uprising followed by the persecution of those who held Jesus Christ above their King as the ultimate authority in matters spiritual. The countryside around Dumfries, Wigtown and Kirkcudbright is replete with memorials to those who were put to death for refusing to renounce their Presbyterian ideals.

Even after the 'Glorious Revolution' of 1688 and the 1707 Union, Galloway's path to peace was not untroubled. When in 1715 the Jacobites rose to return the Stuarts, to the British throne, thousands mobilised to head off the threat to Dumfries. It's no accident that the landowners who held Jacobite sympathies, such as Basil Hamilton of Baldoon and Lady Kenmure, received special attention from the Levellers when they set about their activities less than a decade later.

The quashing of the 1715 finally brought peace to Galloway but the upheavals had exacted a heavy price. Roads and bridges were scarce and the primitive runrig system of farming was ubiquitous. In Roman times and throughout the Middle Ages the land in this part of Scotland had been rich and fertile, but by the 1720s the soil was exhausted – at the very time its inhabitants most needed its bounty to rebuild their society and restore their economic fortunes. Those who'd survived the

'Killing Times' of the seventeenth century were now so poor that they were reported to have scavenged for the black oats left by the horses of King William's army as it passed through Galloway on its way to Ireland and the Battle of the Boyne. For the tenants and cottars, however, matters were about to get much worse.

In 1666 the Scottish and English parliaments had banned the traditional practice of importing cattle from Ireland. Now, post-Union, the South-West was conveniently placed to exploit the expanding cattle trade with Scotland's southern neighbour and, as local historian Alistair Livingston puts it, a few landowners in Wigtownshire had the bright idea of enclosing land to breed beasts for export across the Border. Their motive, he says, was money: 'The advantage was that if you were selling cattle to England you were getting cash. If you were just managing the system on the old traditional basis you were being paid in kind. You were getting your payment of rent in cheese, in milk, in food from the cattle and in grain. So a cash economy was beginning to develop'.

To the lairds of the South-West, who received little from their land, populated as it was by poor tenants and cottars, this was an opportunity not to be missed. Professor Michael Lynch, in his book *Scotland: a New History*, says that before the Union a maximum of thirty thousand cattle a year were driven across the Border to England; by 1750 eighty thousand were exported, and by 1800 the number had risen to one hundred thousand with most of the beasts coming from lands in Galloway.

To make the most of this new cash economy the landowners in this part of Scotland needed to protect these large herds of cattle, and to do this they began erecting stone dykes to enclose their grazing pasture. Once corralled, the herds no longer needed the cowboys or girls to keep track of them and prevent the beasts from wandering amongst the unprotected crops. The fermtouns, with their infield and outfield system of runrigs, became obstacles to the expansionist visions of the landlords. One laird in Kirkinner parish, Sir David Dunbar, created a park more than two miles long and a mile wide on which he kept a thousand or so cattle.

There was no longer any room on the land for the tenants and cottars of Galloway and the customs of the old order of agriculture were simply cast aside by the landowners. The result, says Alistair Livingston, was devastating: 'Essentially they were being driven from the land. They were being cleared from the land – land that their forefathers had inherited for generations. This was an example of the Lowland Clearances, because once these enclosures were built there was no room for the people. There are actually descriptions, from pamphlets of the time, of the poor folks being huddled up along the sides of dykes in the middle of winter with no shelter for themselves, no shelter for their children'.

Many of the cottars and tenants were given notice to leave their farms at Whitsunday, 1723 – up to sixteen families were amongst the first wave of rural refugees. Some emigrated but most were too old or too poor to do so. Their plight is recalled in a ballad written during the Levelling times by James Charters of Dalry:

A generation like to this
Did never man behold,
I mean our great and mighty men
Who covetous are of gold.
Solomon could not well approve
The practice of their lives,
To oppress and to keep down the poor,
Their actions cut like knives.

Among great men where shall ye find
A godly man like Job,
He made the widow's heart to sing,
But our lairds make them sob.
It is the duty of great men
The poor folks to defend,
But worldly interest moves our lairds,
They mind another end.

The lords and lairds they drive us out
From mailings where we dwell,
The poor man says "Where shall we go?"
The rich says "Go to Hell."
These words they spoke in jest and mocks,
But by their works we know,
That if they have their herds and flocks,
They care not where we go.

Against the poor they still prevail
With all their wicked works,
And will enclose both moor and dale
And turn corn fields to parks.

More evidence of the distress and trauma created by these clearances is outlined in an anonymous paper quoted at length in the *Transactions of the Dumfriesshire & Galloway Natural History & Antiquarian Society*. In it the Levellers outline their grievances:

> Every year several tenants are exposed to the mountains, and know not where to get any place; nay it is notourly known some years ago that some of these poor distressed people have, from despair, put hands in themselves and have been found hanged in their own house about the term time when they were obliged to go away and did not

> know where to go, and in a short time no inhabitants will be in all this country . . . the very little town of Minnigaff belonging to Mr Heron [Patrick Heron, laird of Kirroughtree] is only a nest of beggars since he inclosed all the ground about it.

The note goes on to accuse various landlords of not only enclosing their own ground but also renting land from others and clearing that of tenants, too. It goes on:

> This growing evil, which must have the woeful effect of depopulating this country in a very short time, carries these miserable consequences in its bosom, the burghs, trades and corporations which depend on the people of the country, go inevitably to ruin, the parish churches, where the voice of the gospel used to be in purity preached, instead of a numerous auditory, will be left with bare walls, and his Majesty's troops, who ought to be recruited out of the best and most loyal subjects, can expect none out of this country, and we humbly think that the turning a country desolate will be no small encouragement to foreign enemies landing if there should happen a rebellion to bring in to Britain . . . the country being now greatly depopulated through the grievous and extensive inclosures.

Some of the specific allegations against certain landowners were denied at the time by the lairds, but with the benefit of hindsight it is not difficult to see that their decision to enclose grazing pasture and to replace the people with cattle caused significant hardship for those people who since time immemorial had worked and lived off the land they rented but who were now left destitute.

Their suffering was already causing murmurs of discontent amongst the people when they gathered for the annual summer fair at Keltonhill. In 1723, amid the throng of horse and cattle dealers, the tented stalls selling liquor and food and the general clamour of bargaining, carousing and quarrelling there was more serious business to be done. It was here, on the news from Wigtownshire in the west and Glenkens to the north that five hundred families were to be evicted to make way for new cattle parks, that disaffected tenants decided action was necessary. This is where the plan to level the dykes was suggested.

The first moves, however, were not made until the beginning of the following year when two men met in a change house to sign a document pledging each other support in resisting the spread of the hated dykes. Both were tenants faced with eviction because they refused to take on the responsibility for looking after the sub-tenants and cottars removed by their lairds to make way for cattle. One, a man called Robertson, was a tenant on Gordon of Earlston's estate, the other worked part of Lady Kenmure's lands.

Gradually more and more folk gathered to sign the secret bond, and when enough had done so they decided it was time for the first walls to come down. Early targets included the dykes erected by Gordon of Earlston and Lady Kenmure but the gangs of levellers, their ranks swelling all the time, soon moved on, conducting operations across the parishes of Twynholm, Tongland, Kelton and Crossmichael.

They began their deeds under the cloak of darkness but as support grew, so did their courage – and the anxiety of the gentry. In May 1724 James, the 5th Earl of Galloway, wrote from Glasserton to his brother-in-law, Sir John Clerk of Penicuik in Edinburgh, informing him of the 'insolences' of the levellers and urging government intervention:

> . . . you wold hear the insolencies of ane sett of people that have drauen together and destroyed the whole

> encloasours in the Stewartrie, and if we have not the protectione of the Govert by allowing troops to march in the countrie for our assistance, I doe relie belive the whole gentlemen of Galloway will be ruined.

The Earl goes on to recount the experiences of a number of enclosing lairds and confesses:

> [We] don't know how its possible for us to put ane stop to these insolencies if the troops don't assist us. We shall not onlie lose our encloasours but are in hazard of losing our stocks, having noe fences for them, and most goe a drift theough the whole countrie which will be of great disadvantadge then [unless] the outer and the inner of the countrie is not speedlie protected . . .

What added to the fears of the landowners was the highly organised way the gangs of Levellers set about their tasks. Overall leadership, according to contemporary accounts, appears to have been given by a man called Billy Marshall. He became known as the 'King of the Galloway Gypsies' but in his younger days he had been a serving soldier in the Duke of Marlborough's army and had seen action across Europe. It was his practical military knowledge which, in the early days of the revolt, helped forge the Levellers into a formidable force.

Most operations, however, were carried out on a parish-by-parish basis under a chosen captain. Typically they would gather in a company of some forty or so men, women and children. After the loose stones were thrown down, the men would insert poles, between six and eight feet long, into the base or foundation of the wall at key points and on the given command lever the remaining structure to the ground.

The Levellers, though supported by many country people, were not entirely unopposed. Sometimes they would be met at the dyke by others acting for the landowner. One such occasion occurred on the lands owned by Basil Hamilton, where around two thousand Levellers had gathered armed with clubs, pitchforks and guns. A customs officer, James Clerk from Kirkcudbright, relates what happened next:

> About twelve of the clock Mr Basil Hamilton's servants with two or three of this town on horseback advanced to them in order to a Treaty. They were quickly enclosed, dismounted and taken prisoners, and instead of coming to any agreement they were with much difficulty dismissed. The mobb fired three shot upon them in their retreat, then gave the word, "Down with the Dykes", upon which they fell vigorously to work to Mr Hamilton's large dyke, for in the space of three hours they levelled with the ground seven miles of stone dyke in length.

According to Clerk, the country people were now 'wholly loose and resolute, threatening the persons as well as the inclosures of the gentlemen'.

Efforts to deter the 'rabblers' were many and varied but all failed. The reading of the Riot Act, requiring a crowd to disperse, was often countered by the people with quotes from the Solemn League and Covenant protecting the reformed Protestant religion of Scotland.

So while they waited for the troops to arrive, the authorities in Galloway felt they had to act. Under the leadership of the local Stewart Depute, John McDowall, a group of armed landowners and justices of the peace gathered on horseback at the Steps of Tarff to confront the Levellers. They, too, had rallied their supporters and mustered with guns, pistols, swords, hayforks and clubs. The stand-off was described by James Clerk of Kirkcudbright in one of his many letters sent to his brother Sir John Clerk of Penicuik during the Levellers crisis:

> The Stewart Depute, Justices of the peace and Heretors of the Stewartry, met them in a body of about fifty horses well armed and in good order but with no design to attack if the mobb could be brought to reason. After a treaty of peace was negociating four or five hours and that nothing but repeated threats of the mob to fall upon the gentlemen were made, the gentlemen made them offers in general to build no more park dykes and required them to rebuild what they had demolished, then wheeled about and left them, upon which the other party divided themselves into small bodies and went through the country towards this place to finish any kinds of enclosure they could fall on here.

In fact the lairds were divided about whether or not to attack the Levellers. Some were keen to do so but the more cautious views of several among them who had military backgrounds prevailed: the heritors, facing up to a thousand Levellers, were heavily outnumbered and the opposing force, advised by a number of old soldiers, had already taken up the most favourable positions for any battle. Negotiations were the order of the day and a meeting was arranged to 'adjust matters'.

Not for the first time, however, the tenants and cottars were to find the word of their masters and betters less than reliable. They assembled at the pre-arranged meeting place, Bombie Moor, but the landlords failed to show up. Enraged, the Levellers indulged in a fresh bout of dyke demolition and slaughtered cattle. But there was a reason the landlords had ignored the meeting at Bombie Moor. Government troops, in the shape of the Dragoons and the Regiment of Black Horse, had arrived in Galloway ready to crush the revolt.

By early June 1724 six troops of Dragoons were stationed in the area under the command of a French Protestant, Major Du Cary. His first act was to arrest and imprison Robertson – one of the two tenant farmers who had begun the protest at the start of the year – and several other ringleaders. This from another of James Clerk's letters:

> Last night arrived here four troops more of Stair's Dragoons, of which fifty mounted on horseback, so that we now have the whole Regiment but not compleat, by reason of sundry detachments and grass guards. Major Du Cary commands, and designs to encamp hard by.
>
> They have emprisened two in this town who have been active and officious in the affair, and picking up more every day. I believe the troops design to go out in bodys, in search of them [the Levellers] and to attack them, if they find them in number, but their courage is much abated since the arrival of the forces.

The intervention of the Army decisively turned events in favour of the lairds and justices. Over the next four months bands of Levellers were harried across the region, leading to arrests and not a few injuries. James Clerk describes how the troops rode to the rescue of one party of gentry, who, encountering a band of some fifty Levellers, had taken prisoners but who were then attacked by more country people:

> This party of a mob of about fifty were all armed with guns, pitchforks and poles. Upon the gentlemens advancing to them, they kept them off with their pitchforks and clubs. One of them pushed at Mr Basil Hamilton [of Baldoon] with a pitchfork which happened to glance athwart his breast, otherwise if right directed would have prov'd mortall. Another of them struck Mr Heron [Patrick Heron, laird of Kirroughtree] twice with a hanger but was as many times putt off. Another gentleman was almost knockt off his horse, the women all the while plying them with stones, so that they had work enough

> among their hands, and would have come off but indifferently had not the detachment of the Horse immediately come up to their assistance.
>
> As soon as the mobb saw them they made off but the horsemen rode up among them sword in hand, disarmed and took fourteen of them prisoners, one of which had his ear sliced off to a stitch, besides a large cut in the neck.

Such encounters were taking their toll of the Levellers' morale and stamina. According to the *Caledonian Mercury* newspaper: 'It's now taken for granted that the Galloway Levellers are reduced to their marrow bones'.

But attacks on the walls and dykes continued throughout the autumn of 1724, especially in Wigtownshire where, as well as landlords, some of their principal tenants found their cattle maimed and slaughtered. Even the minister at Sorbie, who had ordered a Levellers' manifesto to be taken down from the Kirk doors, found his yard wall mysteriously felled during the night hours.

Despite appearances, however, the Levellers were slowly losing the fight. Records from the *Transactions of the Dumfriesshire & Galloway Natural History & Antiquarian Society* report that their last stand came in October at Duchrae, in the parish of Balmaghie, beside the Black Water of Dee. Here a large number gathered to confront the Dragoons, now led by Major Gardiner following the death of Du Cary.

Weakened by defections, and a lack of will for the fight amongst some, the Levellers were soon defeated by the soldiers. Although the casualties were light, two hundred Levellers were taken prisoner, among them their leader Billy Marshall. He and many of the others were allowed to escape on the march back towards Kirkcudbright and some dyke levelling continued for a time, but as a movement they were finished. Brigadier John Stewart from Sorbie observed when he wrote to Sir John Clerk of Penicuik in November 1724:

> Since my last [letter] they [the Levellers] have not been soe violent upon the dicks [dykes] in genll, but the spirett keeps upp amongst them. They, one Wednesday night last, mett in a considerable body near Whithorne with sythes, pitchfforks and other weapons, killed and houghed Wig's cattle [the laird William Agnew of Castle Wigg] in the inclosure they lately throen doun, but being advertised from the toun that the dragoons were mounting to march upon them they dispersed and severalls of them threw away ther wapons which have been since found.

Remarkable though this revolt by the peasantry was, given Scotland's strict hierarchical social structure, more remarkable still was the impact it had on this society. The actions of the Levellers appeared to split the social ranks above them and prompted considerable fear and alarm far beyond the boundaries of Galloway itself.

The Church sided officially with the landowners. In early May 1724 the Presbytery of Kirkcudbright issued a declaration at Clachanpluck condemning the destruction of the dykes as against the 'institution of heaven' and 'contrair to the word of God' and instructing parishioners to desist from their offensive and grievous practice in 'prejudging the interest of the people'.

Later the same month an Act of the General Assembly of the Church of Scotland, gathering in the nation's capital, thundered against those who levelled the dykes, warning the people of 'the sinfulness and danger of such courses'. The act exhorted them 'speedily to desist therefrom, and required all ministers near to the places where they are assembled, particularly in the bounds of the Synods of Dumfries and Galloway, in the most serious manner, from their pulpits to warn the people of the sinfulness and danger of such actings, and to exhort and obtest them as they have regards of the commands of God, the eternal salvation of their souls as well as the safety of their bodies and families, that they desist from such practices in time coming'.

This was powerful stuff coming from the national church, but many ministers in Kirkcudbright simply refused to read it. Others, according to some of the gentry, actively encouraged the Levellers by railing against the erection of dykes and using their sermons to sympathise with the plight of the dispossessed.

Indeed, from the *Transactions of the Dumfriesshire & Galloway Natural History & Antiquarian Society*, it appears that the Reverend William Falconer, who at the start of the revolt had helped his laird preserve one of his stone dykes at Keltonhill, was arrested in July 1724 and committed to prison in Edinburgh. He was charged, along with another man, with having 'unlawfully convocated themselves with other accomplices, demolished several enclosures in the Stewartry, and continued to the number of twelve or more in a riotous manner after Proclamation against riots had been read to them'.

These divided loyalties were not restricted to the men of God. It also appears that one or two officers of the law were suspected of being levelling sympathisers. In particular, many of the lairds complained about the Stewart Depute, John McDowall.

At the height of the trouble he was called on by Scotland's most senior law officer, the Lord Advocate, to undertake an enquiry into the Levellers' grievances but the heritors were unhappy with the procedures of his commission and wrote to his boss, the Stewart Principal, the Marquis of Annandale. The subsequent exchange of correspondence is illuminating.

Defending his procedures, McDowall explained to the Marquis that he took evidence in open court only from men who, certified by a minister or magistrate, were of good character and that once their testimony was over he allowed the landowner to answer any allegations made against them. But his superior felt this was not good enough. He was worried that the lairds were not being given enough notice of what might be said in open court and was anxious that they should be in a position to object to certain evidence and to challenge their accusers by questioning them during the proceedings.

Further, the Marquis cast doubt on the motives of the Kirk ministers from the Presbytery of Kirkcudbright, holding that their testimony concerning the probity of the character of witnesses was 'of no great account' since they were regarded as 'partial to the common people' and were 'generally looked on as fomenters and encouragers' of the Levellers.

McDowall vigorously defended his impartiality, rejecting the complaints which were prompted by information sent to the Marquis of Annandale by Basil Hamilton of Baldoon – himself regarded by many of the ordinary folk as a Jacobite sympathiser. The Marquis went on to make an extraordinary allegation against a member of his own legal profession, accusing him of being a smuggler:

> It is insinuated that one reason that obliges you to favour these disorderly people so much is that many of them are joined to you in driving a trade of running of goods.

It does seem that contraband brandy was widely available in this part of the world at this time and that many Levellers took the opportunity during their raids to 'liberate' barrels of spirit they claimed the landowner had acquired illegally. Likewise they claimed lairds were continuing to import cattle from Ireland in contravention of the ban imposed by parliament, which was why they often slaughtered beasts as part of their protests.

There is, however, no firm evidence linking McDowall to either of these activities and in his reply to the Marquis he made his outrage plain. It seems to have been enough to make his boss back off. In a letter to Basil Hamilton of 14th September 1724 Annandale argued that further meddling in the commission was unnecessary since the results would be forwarded by McDowall to the Lords of Session in Edinburgh – it seems he was content to let the most senior judges in Scotland decide whether or not the commission had been conducted fairly.

The divisions within Galloway society reflected the propaganda war which was conducted throughout the revolt. The Levellers didn't simply destroy the dykes, they regularly issued pamphlets and declarations justifying their actions and calling for public support – exhortations which were often answered by the landed class in an attempt to influence those in authority elsewhere.

When the Levellers published 'An Account of the Reasons of Some People in Galloway, their Meetings anent Public Grievances through Inclosures', it was followed by an anonymous polemic against the lairds. It was printed in the form of a letter by a poor man to a friend. The writer, while not defending the levelling of dykes, inveighs against the turning of arable land into enclosures for pasturage which he claims are less productive as a result. Although the legal right of a landlord to make improvements to his land is acknowledged, it is argued that these ought to be for the glory of God and for the greater good of human society; that he cannot improve his land to the prejudice or ruin of his fellow creatures – a reference to the clearances and removals of the cottar and tenant families. The scriptures are quoted liberally and, echoing the arguments often used by the Levellers themselves, the author argues that the removal of the dispossessed is prejudicial to good government by depriving it of loyal citizens and making the land vulnerable to a Jacobite enemy.

The letter's contents enraged the gentry, and attempts were made by law officers to prevent further writing about the Levellers' activities. But, soon afterwards, another missive appeared, this time in the nation's capital where news of the revolt in Galloway had been causing concern. Signed by 'Philadelphus', it was entitled 'Opinion of Sir Thomas More, Lord High Chancellor of England concerning enclosures, in answer to a letter from Galloway'.

It, too, was anti-landlord in tone and repeated many of the arguments put forward in the Galloway letter. The question, it said, was not whether a landlord could remove insolvent tenants, nor whether he could improve part of his estate by pasturage – that was not disputed or doubted. The question was, it went on, whether all the proprietors had the power to turn all their grounds into pasturage to the exclusion or oppression of the body of moveable tenants who had a claim by the law of God and nature to be supported by the products of the earth.

It then quoted the judgement of Thomas More, the Lord High Chancellor of England during the time of Henry VIII, on a similar case about lands being taken for the rearing of sheep. More had found against the enclosing of land where people were cast out and rendered destitute, stating: 'Since the increase of pasturage God has punished the avarice of the owners by a rot among the sheep which has destroyed vast numbers of them, but had been more justly laid on the owners themselves'.

An indication of the alarm caused by the pamphlet in Edinburgh was that the Lord Advocate himself went to the bookseller to demand the name of the author. Attempts were made to ban its sale but were doomed to failure. They succeeded only in making it even more popular.

Given the potential for disruption and insurrection these

views represented to the established order, it is perhaps hardly surprising that the authorities could not entertain the possibility of allowing the Levellers' revolt to succeed. And when the perpetrators were eventually defeated and brought to account for their actions, they could expect little in the way of leniency or sympathy from the courts.

Just a glance at the list of those who dispensed justice to the Levellers at the Tolbooth of Kirkcudbright in January 1725 shows how the odds were always stacked against the cottars and tenants who took part in the protests. Thomas Gordon of Earlston, Colonel William Maxwell of Cardoness, John Gordon of Largmore, Robert Gordon of Garvarie, David Lidderdale of Torrs, Nathaniel Gordon of Carlton and John Maxwell, Provost of Kirkcudbright – most, if not all, of those on the bench were landowners and most, if not all, had suffered at the hands of the Levellers.

For those who found themselves prosecuted there was little prospect of legal representation. Many local lawyers were unwilling to take on their cases, some through fear of offending the lairds, others because they were related by family or marriage to them.

Most of the farmers had to rely on the mercy of the court. But they had challenged the power and might of the landed class and now they would have to pay the price. And it was a high one. None was executed – a fate handed out to the rebellious Covenanters of the seventeenth century – but many were imprisoned or banished and the fines handed out were so high that there was never any prospect of a penniless cottar or tenant being able to pay them. Reparation and compensation payments in the order of £400 or £770 Scots, even shared among more than just those convicted in court, were stratospheric sums which sent a message far and wide to those who contemplated insurrection.

The suppression of the Galloway Levellers had consequences far beyond the individuals concerned. As the lairds resumed their enclosing activities, many of those displaced emigrated and, in time, the fondness for erecting dykes spread to the councils of whole burghs: less than a year after the revolt was put down, the Royal Burgh of Wigtown decided to enclose its own lands in the interests of its citizens.

By the time the Lowland Clearances began in earnest some forty years later, the lessons of the rising in Galloway had been well heeded by the authorities. In future the landowners pursued their revolution within the confines of the lease system, encouraging those tenants who adopted the new farming ways but making it impossible for those who did not to remain on the land. They were also careful to ensure that those who were removed were provided with somewhere to go and some kind of alternative way to earn a living; they were not left, like the cottars of Galloway, to shiver without shelter at the side of the dykes which had banished them from their farms.

This, perhaps, is why history records no other uprising of a similar scale to the Galloway revolt during the course of the Agricultural Revolution despite its significant consequences for the majority of the rural population. That doesn't mean there weren't other symptoms of unrest, or that Scots meekly accepted the changes pursued by the lowland lairds – indeed, a spirited debate is emerging amongst Scotland's historians over the extent of protest against the improvements.

Professor Chris Whatley of Dundee University says Galloway was a one-off in scale but there were other instances of anti-enclosure disturbances: 'One of the reasons why there were fewer of these disturbances in Scotland was partly because the Galloway levelling activities had been so frightening for the authorities that they took care to ensure that that sort of thing shouldn't happen again. A lot of the activities of landowners in the second half of the eighteenth century are designed to preclude, to pre-empt this sort of activity. That's one reason why people were re-housed and not just thrown off the land. An alternative was created to pacify people'. Although forcible evictions were by no means unknown, the Lowland lairds, unlike their counterparts in the Highlands during the nineteenth century, rarely needed to resort to them.

The proximity of its lands to the English border and the lucrative trade in cattle meant that Galloway was among the first regions of Scotland to be exposed to the full rigours and demands of the free market. It would not be the last, and wherever the pressures of population and commerce grew, so did the ambitions of the improving lairds who stood to gain. The losers, all too often, were the cottars and the poor and struggling tenants and sub-tenants whose hold on the land was so fragile.

CHAPTER FOUR

Winners and Losers

> 'My sense from the sources is that in the later eighteenth century the actual loss of land, let's take aside forcible removal, the simple fact of losing land and becoming landless was much more significant for larger numbers of people in lowland society than it was in the Gaeltachd.'
>
> Professor Tom Devine

The imposing Palladian structure of Paxton House, almost literally a stone's throw from the English border, is a statement of the power and prestige of the Homes of Wedderburn. It was built in the late 1750s on the banks of the meandering River Tweed, a few miles inland from Berwick. What a contrast those languid waters must have been to the frenetic activity that suddenly burst upon the county as the stone walls and panelled rooms of Paxton were thrust skywards. Paxton was a metaphor for what was going on elsewhere across Berwickshire. Elsewhere indeed across the southern Lowlands. The very time of its construction was the moment when an agricultural revolution began in Scotland. It was also the starting point for the Lowland Clearances.

The flatlands and rich soil of the Merse, retarded and underdeveloped since the fourteenth century because of the Anglo-Scottish wars, was at last ripe for improvement. But it took innovation, capital and political power to push the changes through. As late as 1724 Berwickshire was a bleak place. The English traveller and writer Daniel Defoe described in his journal how, when he crossed the Border from England, he at once entered the wasteland of Coldingham Moor:

> Upon which, for about eight miles, you see hardly a hedge, or a tree, except in one part, and that at a good distance, nor do you meet with but one house in all the way, and that no house of entertainment, which was thought was but poor reception for Scotland to give her neighbours, who were strangers at the very entrance to her bounds.

Within forty years this mixture of worthless scrub, moor, forest and bog had been transformed into Scotland's bread-basket. Berwickshire was in the van of agricultural improvement. Large, productive, regular fields replaced the plasticine slithers of runrig. New roads and bridges were constructed to transport the ever-increasing bounty from the land to the urban markets of central Scotland and northern England. The landowners, or heritors, even considered laying out a canal to link the inland fields to the coast. Leading the way were the Homes of Wedderburn, at the apex of the social pyramid, and still wielding almost total power over the people.

It is a great myth of Scottish history that it was only the Highland chiefs who lived like mini-kings in their own fiefdoms. Most Lowland aristocrats held sway in the same fashion right through to the end of the eighteenth century, and in the case of the Homes well into the nineteenth. Like the Highland chiefs, their grip was rooted in military power. The Crown depended on this for effective local government in the shires, and as a source of men and money during war and civil crisis.

The Wedderburns had been Wardens of the East March since medieval days. Successive lairds called to arms their border 'tail' in battles that resonate through Scotland's history. Unhappily for the Homes, and more especially for those unfortunates dragooned into their ranks, they habitually picked the losing side. The 4th Lord died at Flodden in 1513; the 5th perished at the Battle of Pinkie in 1547; while the 6th sided with Mary Queen of Scots at her disastrous dénouement of Langside in 1568. The 7th gave in to requests for cash from James VI and almost bankrupted the family, while the 8th laird, along with his son, was amongst three thousand Scots slaughtered by Cromwell at the Battle of Dunbar in 1650.

Yet kinship and ties of fealty, however unpropitious the cause, still led the 10th Laird of Wedderburn to raise a force for the unhappy House of Stuart when their standard was hoisted in 1715. This, too, almost ended in disaster – George Home only escaped with his neck intact after some nifty political string-pulling. Nothing could be done for his brother Frances who was marched off to Liverpool and sold into slavery in North America. For once, though, luck was with the Homes. A cousin purchased Frances' freedom, and when he arrived at the Chesapeake as a free man he decided to give the colonies a try. In later life Frances Home became tutor to the young George Washington and might legitimately claim some credit for shaping the character of the great revolutionary general and first President of the United States.

Back home, the crushing of the Jacobite rising gave the Wedderburns, and many other lairds, plenty to think about. It was time to be done with fighting. The cause of the Stuarts was over, as was that of Scottish independence, though it would be many decades before there was any significant interference in the daily affairs of the Northern Kingdom.

Local government remained firmly in the hands of the great families. Whatever nostalgic yearnings there might have been for the past, and in spite of the further Jacobite distraction of 1745, Scotland's future was now settled. It lay in Union with Westminster and peace along the Border. Those with vision would also have seen the opportunities for trade and money-making not just in England but with her ever-growing colonial possessions. Ironically it had been Scotland's attempt at empire-building, culminating in the 1690s disaster of Darien in central America, that had made Union all but inevitable.

In Berwickshire, the power of the Homes would henceforth be measured not in the strength of their private army, but in the way they lived. Conspicuous consumption meant all the trappings of a luxurious dwelling in the country and a fine townhouse in London, grand clothes, lavish foreign trips and an education for the children which was well away from the common bairns at the parish school of Paxton. The wealth of their lands would deliver a cash crop to underpin all of this. That future, however, would scarcely have seemed credible to the 10th Laird as he languished in a London jail in 1716.

When George Home swept out from his Berwickshire fastness to answer the call of the Old Pretender, the Wedderburns actually owned just a thousand acres. They claimed feudal superiority over a much larger portion of the county, but legally they were not major landholders. How, then, did the Homes turn the disastrous defeat of 1715, when the family was all but ruined, into the glory and riches of Paxton and the vast estates they came to hold by the second half of the eighteenth century? In part at least they played the system. As well as taking the lead from agricultural innovators like John Cockburn of Ormiston – just up the road in East Lothian – they also appropriated huge chunks of formerly common land. And they did it wholly within the law.

The Wedderburn experience was not unique. They were not the first minor aristocrats to grab land, and the methods they employed would hardly have seemed out of place. But their appropriation of the common of Billie in the north of Berwickshire allowed for the opening up of the Merse. The Homes were instrumental in enclosing their estates, draining and liming the land, sowing new crops and adopting English methods of rotation. Twenty years after Daniel Defoe's visit,

Berwickshire was a very different place. He would have been hard pushed to recognise it.

The overall effect was to accelerate the fortunes of the Wedderburns. But the motivation was not simply money and family aggrandisement, though these were, of course, welcome consequences. Lairds embraced change from a combination of need, patriotism, and, however bizarre to the modern mind, of science. Some moved quickly, others slowly, and others still hardly at all. The haphazard and piecemeal nature of the improvements disguised what was going on all over the Scottish lowlands. They blurred the big picture and may have weakened any opposition. But the result was nothing less than a true agricultural revolution which consumed the countryside at breakneck speed.

That is not to say that pre-Union Scotland was static. Professor Tom Devine has charted a movement away from multiple tenancies and towards written legal leases which seems to have begun to take hold in some areas by the late seventeenth century. This is particularly the case in the South-East where the demands of the Edinburgh market combined with good soil and suitable terrain. Rents in this part of the country were paid, not in kind, but in cash. Farms, though ostensibly still traditional, were already moving away from several units of runrig to fewer, occasionally single, occupancies. There was a consequent reduction in the number of small tenants in each unit. Work was still to be had on the land, but for those who lost out in this early part of the process, the soil could no longer be considered their own. In Lothian and around southern Scotland some of the cottar population were part peasant, part proletarian wage-slave even before 1707. The scene was set and the conditions favourable for the rapid transformation of rural society.

From the early 1760s Scotland's population, unchecked by war or famine, leapt upwards. The rise in itself was scarcely dramatic, but the distinctive feature of the increase was where it was felt. Villages became towns and towns became cities at an incredible pace. Whereas in 1700 only one in ten of the population lived in communities of 2,000 people or more, by 1821 that figure was one in three. These new urban centres drove the industrial revolution which has provided the enduring image of west-central Scotland ever since.

Like the water wheels which powered the new mills, the start was slow but then a momentum took over. Again, in a perfect circle, the populace of these new communities had to be fed, and that prompted innovation in the fields which, in turn, required fewer people on the land and fuelled the drift to the towns.

The pace of improvement in some areas was seismic. Professor Devine, who has extensively charted the landholding structure in Lanarkshire, found that multiple tenancies on the Douglas estate fell from 64 per cent in the 1730s to just 16 per cent two decades later. Though substantial, this was not unique. Throughout the Lowlands, and beginning first in the south and in Lothian and then spreading northwards, lairds began to reorder their affairs.

Excluding innovators like Cockburn and Grant, this reorganisation was carried out in the main by factors. Who won and who lost was a game of rural roulette. The most willing and able tenants were rewarded with longer leases and more land – land which was taken from others who were considered in a less favourable light. In this way an embryonic capitalist tenant-farmer class began to emerge – a social grouping which had a huge stake in making the changes successful.

It was all about carrot and stick. The incentive was a lease or tack; the fear was loss of tenure at the end of the now accepted written terms of that arrangement. Increasingly these leases included conditions relating to improvement. Failure to carry them through could see a family dispossessed regardless of how long they had worked the farm or how much they had bettered it for the laird. Even strict adherence to the improving clauses carried no guarantees of extension. Professor Devine has uncovered the following regulations drawn up by John Burrell, factor for the Duke of Hamilton's estates, in 1764:

> That the tenants within the Baronys of Hamilton, Cambuslang and Dalserf shall be restricted first from ploughing above one third part of their present possessions; second Never to take up ground without lime or some other manure; third Never to take above three crops running; Fourth that all ground shall be richly laid down with clover and rygrass seeds; three good crops of grain and six good crops of grass alternately. Any tenant who acts in a contrary way shall be liable in double rent for the ground otherways cropped.

By the latter part of the eighteenth century these improving leases were standard across much of the Lowlands. They had been accepted, although as William Aiton reflected in his *Agricultural Report for Ayrshire* in 1811, they had not been welcomed at the time:

> In the parish of Kilmarnock . . . the popular prejudice and extraordinary clamour among the tenantry against these innovations was very strong. Restricting the tillage to one third of the possession was remonstrated against, as an encroachment on the liberties of the people . . . The tenants were disposed to consider every improvement they were required to make on their possessions, as tending only to augment their labour, and increase the rent rolls of the proprietors.

Certainly rental income rose and in some cases rose spectacularly. Taking the example of the Douglas estates in Lanarkshire, rents increased from £1,426 in 1737 to almost £9,000 in

1815. It was a similar story on the Earl of Eglinton's lands in Ayrshire, the Duke of Hamilton's possessions across many parts of central Scotland and on virtually every other lowland estate which has been surveyed.

Tenants copied tenants, improving leases made the land more bountiful and the towns' populations swelled. Little wonder, then, that history has remembered this era an 'Age of Improvement'. Scotland was changed forever. But what happened to the people who struggled to adapt?

Those who could not pay the increased rents were obliged to leave lands their families had lived and worked on for decades if not centuries. Those who could not deliver the improvements of a given lease were also obliged to leave. Those who were not offered a new lease at the end of a set term were likewise given no option to stay. This was, in the words of Tom Devine, 'clearance by stealth'.

There is no known lowland equivalent of the wholesale removal of communities in the manner carried out by Patrick Sellar in Strathnaver in 1815 and which characterises the Highland Clearances. But hundreds of fermtouns, mapped in the seventeenth century, were gone by the time Sellar was at work in Sutherland. Some were ancient; Lour in Peeblesshire, for example, had a history which has been traced back to the Iron Age.

Very little work has been done on fermtouns. Even the designation is a mystery to most Scots. Perhaps this is because the physical remains are sparse. The buildings scarcely consisted of anything more than layers of turf on top of a base of stone. When the people were moved out, this aggregate was recycled to build dykes which enclosed the fields or as material for the new farmhouses and byres. Two-and-a-half centuries on there is little to mark out the fermtoun sites from the rest of the landscape.

The names of some of these communities have lived on,

however. Across the Lowlands large farms which were created from the amalgamation of the tiny holdings habitually kept the name of the former settlement. Jan Blaeu's 1654 *Atlas Novus* (*New Atlas*) was based on the remarkable cartography of Timothy Pont between 1583 and 1596 and it provides a detailed picture of the spread of the settlements across the countryside, areas which contemporary maps show as bare and empty.

Lour, a mile or so south from the village of Stobo, stands about 250 feet above the River Tweed on an upland incline of the valley. It was an ideal location for defence, which is doubtless why the community endured for so long. A Roman encampment has been uncovered four miles away though it would seem that locals traded with rather than fought against those particular invaders. How they coped in the centuries of Anglo-Scottish warfare, being bang in the middle of the debatable lands, is less clear, but Lour was certainly identified by Blaeu, and the names of some of the seventeenth-century inhabitants have also been preserved.

The site was excavated in the late 1950s and has continued to interest amateur archaeologists such as Ed Archer. Without his trained eye, the trek to the top of the hill would have been unremarkable. But Ed pointed out a collection of raised mounds, centred around a long house, perpendicular to some undulating furrows – evidence of runrigs which would have been naturally drained by the slopes of the hill.

Life was hard here, as it was for subsistence farmers everywhere in Scotland. But it was a settled existence. Then, suddenly, the landowner decided to reorganise his estate, move the people off and bring in the more profitable commodity of sheep. 'This was evidence of the lowland clearances', according to Ed Archer. 'It's a very early example of lowland clearance because we have evidence that this estate was split up as early as 1742.' Four years before Culloden the death knell for an old system was sounded two hundred miles to the south of Drumossie Moor.

In 1767 an Edinburgh lawyer called Montgomerie took over the lands of Lour and 'rationalised' things still further. It was the end for the fermtoun which, by the 1790s, had ceased to exist.

The vista south from the ruins of the fermtoun is a desolate one. Unchanged from medieval times, this is the old Scotland. To the north is the pleasant aspect of improvement. The Montgomeries and their factors laid out rectangular fields, grass parklands, planned forests and avenues. And in 1811, as an opulent replacement for the peel tower, Stobo Castle – now Stobo Castle Health Farm – was finished. This is the new Scotland: a man-made creation, conceived in a big idea of the mid-eighteenth century and replicated hundreds of times over in the period between 1760 and 1830. Like Lour, the evidence is there. It's just waiting to be discovered.

There is no record of how the cottars of Lour reacted to the news that they were to leave. Perhaps they were pleased. The winters of 1740 and 1741 had been harsh, so the prospect of life in a new village or simply away from the drudgery of the land might well have appealed. It is impossible to specify how much weight should be given to 'pull' and how much to 'push' factors. But that question could equally be asked of much of the population drift from the Highlands.

Having traced the summons of removal through sheriff courts, Professor Devine believes there was a significant increase in evictions, especially in the upland areas of Lanarkshire, Perthshire, Stirlingshire, Angus, Moray and Aberdeenshire in the 1760s and 1770s. Undoubtedly some people would have left of their own accord. 'That said,' concludes Professor Devine, 'we cannot explain the catastrophic haemorrhage of population in some of these rural areas over such short time spans except by suggesting that either indirect or direct compulsion was used. And above all it is very difficult to explain how a social tier of the countryside, an entire social echelon of the Scottish countryside, which had existed for centuries – namely the cottar elements in rural lowland society – suddenly move off the land in their entirety. I find it very hard to accept that that could have been achieved simply by a new wave of mass voluntarism, eager to take advantage of some opportunities at a distance or outside the immediate neighbourhood'.

There can be no doubt that to some the towns were indeed attractive, especially to the younger sons and daughters who had no hope of being granted a tenancy. Professor Christopher Whatley says that industrialisation was 'roaring ahead in Scotland from about the 1760s and the 1770s', providing opportunities for those who were no longer able to sustain themselves solely on the land.

Whatley identified the village of Stanley in Perthshire, now a sleepy community on the banks of the Tay, as a prime example of industrial development working hand-in-glove with rural change. It was here in the late eighteenth century that the talents of the great English cotton master Richard Arkwright were married to the needs of the Duke of Atholl. Atholl had been clearing people from his southern Perthshire estates as he pursued a vigorous programme of agricultural improvement along the model provided in Lothian and the Borders. Perhaps from a sense of paternalism, or perhaps for more commercial reasons, Atholl was anxious to retain as many of his tenants as possible. Harvesting was still labour-intensive, so to lose the people altogether would have worked against the interests of the new farms. Arkwright's mill complex, built along the fast-flowing waters of the River Tay, provided a neat solution to all of the problems. Well, almost all. Those erstwhile peasant cottars who now had no place on the land were given accommodation at Stanley and jobs at the mill. The profits from the mill, and the rents from the cottages, went to the estate. The people were retained as a reservoir of labour for the farms.

In this way and across Scotland people moved from the land into industry. If there was no mill nearby, then they could become outworkers for the linen trade, or colliers in the mines, or they could seek out opportunities in the cities. The displaced of the Lowland Clearances had choices. The one choice denied to them, however, was that of staying where they were and doing what they had always done.

Professor Whatley believes much of the urban protest which developed in Scotland in this period was rooted in the upheavals in the countryside: 'Many former country people found it difficult to adapt to life in the towns, mainly because what this required was continuous supervised work. No longer were you working with the season, no longer were you picking and choosing what hours you worked. Your working day was driven by the mill machinery. One of the great challenges of living in a place like Stanley was that people who had formerly been cottars or sub-tenants were now wholly dependent on their money wage for their subsistence, and a consequence of that was that when wages were not enough, or when the payment of those wages was stopped because of a stoppage at the mill, or the price of food rose, these communities were in great difficulties because they had become wage workers'.

For those who remained on the land, life was now very different. Alexander Somerville's ancestors had been subtenants in the parish of Muckhart in the Ochils. It was on marginal upland and sometime after his father's birth in 1760 that they were evicted from a place called Nether-aichlin-Sky. 'Who were the last of our family in it I do not know,' wrote Somerville in his 1848 *Autobiography of a Working Man*, 'but all the sons and daughters were scattered to the world in early life to work for the means of life elsewhere, the little farm being added to others to make a large farm.'

Somerville provides eloquent testimony to the struggle of the common man. While Burns eulogises the nobility of labour in the 'Cottar's Saturday Night', this *Autobiography of a Working Man* provides a more brutal and perhaps more realistic picture of what life was like for those who lost their lands. Once evicted, Somerville's father became a carter in Alloa but was again left destitute when his horse died. James Somerville then returned to the land but this time as a day labourer, moving around the country and hiring himself out at feeing fairs. He eventually arrived in Berwickshire where he married a local girl. Many bairns followed, including Alexander, born near Ayton in 1811:

> When we lived in Springfield the house rent was paid by finding one shearer for the harvest. My mother did that all the winter before I was born and the winter after, besides shearing in the harvest time – the hours being in harvest between sun and sun. The stack carrying was done thus: Two women had a barrow made of two poles, with canvass stretched between the poles; upon which canvass were laid 10 or 12 sheaves. The two women then carried that load through the yard and up a gangway to the upper floor of the barn, meeting another couple going down empty. They laid down their barrow, and rolled the sheaves out of it on the floor, where another woman was 'loosing out' and laying the loosened sheaves on a table, where the man who 'fed in' to the mill stood. One woman stood on the stack outside and she forked down the sheaves to the ground; while another on the ground assisted to load the woman who carried the barrows. At this work and in the harvest field did my mother bear the burden of heavy labour

> and of me. After I was born I was carried to her to be suckled.
>
> Should you ever be in Scotland and see Springfield, you will find a row of shabby looking tiled sheds, the centre of which is about 12 feet by 14, and not so high in the walls as to allow a man to get in without stooping. That place without ceiling, or anything beneath the bare tiles of the roof; without a floor save the common clay; without a cupboard or recess of any kind; with no grate but the iron bars which the tennants carried to it, built up and took away when they left it; with no partition of any kind save what the beds made; with no window save four small panes on one side – it was this house for which, to obtain leave to live in, my mother sheared the harvest and carried the stacks.

Here was the bleak reality of the 'Age of Improvement' for countless thousands who lost their toehold on the soil. For the landless lowlanders there was at least work to be had, and Professor Smout's assessment that 'almost certainly they were no worse off' in a material fashion is doubtless correct.

Families swapped clay-wattle hovels for brick-and-tile shelters; they probably ate better, wore slightly better clothes and perhaps lived a little longer. But did that mean people were happy with the changes? Did that imply acceptance, whether passive or active? As Dr Jim Hunter says, the same point could be made when coldly assessing the implications of the forced removal of crofters from their Highland hovels.

The 'unintended consequences' of clearance, whether by stealth in the refusal to renew a lease in the Lowlands or through brutal eviction in the Highlands, might well have led to betterment in the long run. In most cases that's exactly what happened. Dr Hunter tells the story of a Crofters' Union meeting a few years ago on a stormy winter's night on Skye.

One man, drenched from lashing rain, shook off his oilskins at the entrance to the hall. 'The clearances,' he shouted, 'didn't go far enough. I could be growing oranges in California!' A joke, of course, but one which, even given the decades which have passed, some will still consider to be in bad taste. Yet the point is well made.

For those whom fate smiled upon, life in the new, improved lowland Scotland could still be painfully hard. Purchasing land in an age of rigid hierarchy was all but impossible. By the late eighteenth century there was none to be had. All the commonalties had been seized and parcelled out amongst the heritors. The very best that a tenant-farmer could hope for was a lease, and then an extension to that lease. Attached to the contract were conditions of improvement. This was how Scotland was changed. Tenants were instructed to bring in new land, to drain marsh and bog, to plough out stones, to uproot ancient trees, to create a new Eden from the wilderness. It was back-breaking and it was heartbreaking, because come the end of a lease, once the land had been tamed, the farm was obviously worth more and often consolidated into a larger farm. Lairds and their factors might have played the paternalist role, but what really mattered was money. And a lot of money was being made. Alexander Lowe, in his survey of Berwickshire in 1794, observed:

> The spirit of Improvement in this county is very general . . . By a vigorous pursuit in the improvements of husbandry, in the course of four or five years one estate rose in rent from £500 to £1,200; another £500 to £1,500 a year.

The gentry of Berwickshire, said Lowe, had:

> First set going the improved plan of a rational system of agriculture, which at the present time is not inferior to

> any other county of Britain. They granted favourable leases to tenants, abolishing the oppressive servitudes hitherto existing, enclosed, built steadings, convenient and useful and spared no kind of expense in encouraging the industrious, active farmer.

By the time of Lowe's tribute to the gentry of the Borders, like-minded individuals were carrying through the same improvements all the way to Inverness-shire. On the slopes of Kiltarlity, with an outlook towards the Black Isle, Dr Jim Hunter has traced a remarkable process. The same people pushed cultivation up the sides of the hills, being successively deprived of their farms and then granted a lease to 'take-in' more ground further up the slopes. To this day the better farms are on the lower levels while conifers near the summit mark the limit of human endeavour.

From the margins of Berwickshire to the Buchan hinterland, progress struck home. One of the last parts of lowland Scotland to be affected was rural Aberdeenshire. The events were chronicled in the memoirs of Christian Watt, born in the Broadsea district of Fraserburgh in 1833. This is how she described 'the making of the big farms':

> The whole world changed. It was not gradual but sudden, like lightning. Whole gangs of men came to reclaim the land, they ploughed bogs and stanks, everywhere was the smell of burning whins. Suddenly huge parks were marching up the side of Mormond hill, so greedy did they become for land . . . You could make a bit of money at drystane dyking if you had the skill, for all the parks were enclosed. New steadings and farm houses were going up everywhere . . . In the new order the cottar was hit hardest. Formerly he was a tenant at will with the same rights as a free man, for he could sell his little holding or leave it to his son. Now he was a slave . . . I often wonder

> what brought it all to a head so that so radical a change could take place. A lot of money was coming in at the expense of the freedman and cottar, who were being paid with sweeties in return for their labour.

Somerville and Watt paint a picture far removed from any rural idyll. Their testimony, which gives a voice to the victims of the clearances, is backed up by the monumental findings of the Old Statistical Account. They roar the consequences of change. Most echoed the sentiments of Alexander Lowe that Scotland, at long last, was in the vanguard of progress. Rev. William Simson of Gordon, for example, spoke of how:

> The roads to Berwick and Eyemouth were, until lately, in a bad state; but now they are in good repair. The principal crossroads in the parish are also much improved. All these roads do great honour to the public support of the gentlemen who planned and promoted them.

These roads fairly hummed to the tune of commerce. By the mid-1790s, 40,000 bolls of grain were being moved across Berwickshire to fill the holds of trading luggers in the newly extended harbour at Eyemouth. Scotland was no longer a country which struggled to feed its own small populace in times of hardship. It was now producing huge surpluses which were traded across the United Kingdom and overseas.

But the highways which were replacing dirt tracks and rutted lanes also provided exit points for people, as John Renton, heritor of Chesterbank, bemoaned when charting the parish of Coldingham:

> Our supernumerary men go partly to England, and partly to Edinburgh and other populous towns in Scotland in quest of employment.

The message from many of the contributors to the Old Statistical Account of the 1790s and a message which echoed from lowland parish to lowland parish was one of depopulation: the loss of people; the destruction of cottages; the ending of a way of life:

> Villages have been demolished and land, which formerly gave sufficient employment to three or four families has been put into the possession of one man. Rents have been raised beyond what the ability of the tenants could pay, who have thus been made bankrupt, driven from their farms.
> Mr John Naismith, Parish of Hamilton, Lanarkshire.

> The causes of depopulation in this parish may be these: Formerly this parish was divided into small farms, and each farmer kept several cottages; but now the farms are much enlarged, and the farmers seem to have imbibed a strong prejudice against all cottages, pulling down some of them every year.
> Rev. James Maconochie, Parish of Dolphinton, Peebles-shire.

> The population in 1755 was 1,102 souls, in 1791 it was 740 . . . Each of these parishes seems to have been as populous 50 or 60 years ago as the united parish is now. The decrease is entirely accounted for from one farmer now occupying what several had occupied formerly; from arable land being converted into store or sheep farms; from a greater number of cattle and horse being reared; and from people of late years, particularly young persons, removing to places where there are manufactures and public works.
> Rev. Joseph Henderson, united parishes of Wistoun and Robertoun, Lanarkshire.

In almost every part of the parish ruins of dwelling-house are seen; and the small farms which belonged to these, annexed to others.
Rev. Thomas Brown, Parish of Inverkip, Renfrewshire.

The population is considerably decreased in the memory of the present inhabitants. The reason assigned is the common one of converting several of the small farms into a large one.
Rev. William Brown, Eskdalemuir, Dumfriesshire.

The number of families is thought to be considerably smaller than it was twenty years ago . . . since improvements in agriculture began, some of the farmers occupy more land than their predecessors; for they think a small farm will not defray the expense of management. For this land they pay a very considerably advanced rent, and are at a much more considerable expense in improving it. The farmer, therefore, cannot let a small parcel of land, and keep a cow, to a tradesman or mechanic, upon terms near so low as formerly. The tradesman grudges to pay what the farmer thinks his accommodation worth. The consequence is, the tradesman retires to a town or village, and the farmer tills his own fields.
Rev. Patrick Stewart, Parish of Kinneff, Kincardineshire.

The obvious cause of the decrease of population has been the throwing down of the principal estates into grass farms which are now in the hands of a few considerable dealers in cattle.
Rev. Thomas Scott, Parish of Ballingry, County of Fife.

The taste for enlarging and uniting farms forces the people from the healthy employment of a country life

> to take refuge in manufacturing towns and populous cities which may literally be said to be the graves of the human species.
>
> Rev. John Scott, Parish of Auchertoul, County of Fife.

At the start of this process, around 1760, Scotland was a hierarchical country, but it was not a nation of classes. Rather there were strata within society. That had changed by the time the Old Statistical Account was compiled. By 1830, when the transformation of lowland Scotland was complete, a class system had become entrenched. By then the number of tenant-farmers had been, to use the epithet of another minister-contributor, 'thinned'. The sub-tenants, or cottars, had disappeared from the countryside – yet they had once made up between a quarter and a third of the population of some parishes. These were the detritus of the Agricultural Revolution: the peasants who became paid day labourers or who stoked the engines of industry in the new towns.

Even those who managed to win and keep a lease experienced hard times, but they were becoming the middle class in Scottish rural society. Above them were the landowners, the elite who prospered and who spent their new-found wealth giving work to great architects like James and Robert Adam. Their mansions, including Mellerstain in Berwickshire and Culzean in Ayrshire, are sumptuous contrasts to the draughty castles they replaced.

The substantial lowland lords had already distanced themselves from the common folk by 1760. But this was now accentuated and accelerated. The fashion was for a proper education in England. The need was for a second house in London, and perhaps a third in Edinburgh too. The vogue was to embrace English Episcopal worship and to develop a taste for expensive art, furnishings and garb.

For many great lords Scotland became less of a home than a

holiday spot. Their estates, which now had to produce more and more cash, were run by factors. The Duke of Hamilton might have thought of himself as a paternalist, but how much did he know of what was actually taking place on his estates or what the fate was of the people who lived there?

Paxton House, another of the Adams' creations, was a commission for the Homes of Wedderburn in 1758. A family which had nearly been ruined through a dalliance with Jacobitism was, within forty years, awash with assets and brimful of confidence for the future. Patrick Home, the great-nephew of the laird who almost stepped on to the gallows in London, was able to take the 'Grand Tour of Europe' and became engaged to – though he never married – a courtier of Frederick the Great of Prussia.

Succeeding to the Wedderburn lands and title, Patrick engineered his own election as an MP, basing himself for lengthy periods at Westminster. There was a house in Bedford Square and, of course, the luxury of Paxton House. How was all this achieved? Simple, according to his descendant, John Home-Robertson: 'He would have needed money and that was coming out of the land here in Berwickshire'.

Estate correspondence shows that Patrick Home, even while he was away from home, retained a keen interest in the development of Berwickshire. He oversaw the laying out of bridges and roads and further refinements in crop development and the allocation of leases.

In the 1790s there was a concern that progress was being impeded because some tenants could make more money from the cocaine trafficking of the day – the hugely lucrative trade in smuggled whisky and wine. The feeling was that the land was suffering as a result, and George Home of Gunsgreen wrote to the laird that one tenant 'has taken to smuggling and deserted his farm . . . There is this disadvantage in new improven lands. That if they are not indisciously (sic) and even tenderly managed they suffer an injury that cannot be repaired without a considerable expense'.

Wedderburn, as an improving laird, certainly expended large sums on his policies. But the returns were great indeed. As John Home-Robertson concludes, the actions and directions of the landed class totally transformed a nation: 'What happened in the eighteenth century with the enclosures and the improvements and the creation of new big farms in place of common grazing completely altered the landscape of Scotland. The production of food, the more efficient production of crops allowed the population to increase and added to the wealth and the prosperity of the nation of Scotland and indeed the United Kingdom. It changed, forever, the landscape. What we take for granted is this patchwork of fields and hedges and trees and walls. But that was created in the eighteenth century. Before then it would have been open scrubland'.

CHAPTER FIVE

Enlightened Improvement

> 'The landowners believed that the main point of planning a village that would incidentally make people happy and virtuous was that by doing so their own profits would be increased, and their own hold on leadership of society thereby confirmed and strengthened.'
>
> Professor T.C. Smout, 'The Landowner and the Planned Village in Scotland, 1730–1830'

It was not hard to spot those who were thriving in the new commercial world ushered in by the revolution in agriculture. The isolated stone-built farmsteads of the new capitalist class of tenant-farmers gazed out over wide expanses of fields neatly divided and fenced off to public access by the new enclosures. Here the freshly limed soil and strictly rotated crops of root vegetables, grasses and clover yielded bigger harvests and gave a different look to the rural surroundings. The old fermtouns were gone, and where people once eked out a living from their runrigs, cattle or sheep now grazed over a silent landscape. Every so often from the midst of the countryside arose the grand buildings and mansions of the architects of all this change.

For the landowners of lowland Scotland the new wealth provided by their enclosed estates was evidence enough of the virtue of the improvements. They forged ahead with further investment, spending huge sums. The Homes of Wedderburn in Berwickshire were not alone in investing heavily in the new agriculture. Documents uncovered by Tom Devine in his book, *The Transformation of Rural Scotland*, show that in the five years from 1771 the Earl of Strathmore spent more than £22,000 on enclosing and draining land and building new roads and bridges in Angus. Richard Oswald's outlay on his lands in Ayrshire was more than £2,000 in just six months, and between 1805 and 1812 the estate of Bonnytown near St Andrews attracted investment of £10,000. Its own records show how the money was spent:

> The lands have been completely drained, enclosed and subdivided, with substantial stone dykes, an excellent modern farm steading built; the mansion house repaired and additions made to it, so as to render it a comfortable place of residence, and about twenty acres of the lands planted. The whole has been completely limed and dunged, so that the lands are at present in the very best possible order.

This new age of rapid activity and growth created a problem for the lairds, however. As Professor Devine observes: 'One of the ironies of the Agricultural Revolution is that it was not a technological revolution. It was driven forward by labour-intensive methods; it was the sweat of the people that was important, it was their muscle that was important. So building up the new estate roads, creating the enclosures, even harvesting the increased crop required increased labour'.

But to create their new cattle ranches or crop plains the landlords had removed the people who once lived on their land. The tenants and cottars who were cleared had moved to the burghs of barony and the rural hamlets which were now growing quickly across the Lowlands. These villages and settlements – along with the swiftly expanding towns and cities – were soaking up the displaced and the landless.

The explosion in Scotland's population which was helping

to fuel the growth of these places was in turn creating greater demand and a bigger market for all that the new commercial farms could produce. This meant the lairds still needed their former tenants and cottars – not as farmers but as hired labourers, especially at the busiest time of year when the crops had to be harvested.

The planned village was a uniquely Scottish solution to this problem of what to do with a population whose removal from the land was required by the new revolution in agriculture but whose services were still needed to carry it forward. Professor Chris Smout, an expert on the development of the planned villages, says they were important not only because they were the places where a lot of the people who were displaced by rural change ended up; they also helped landowners retain people on their estates: 'The population might have declined for other reasons but the general ambition of the landowner was to have his people around him. It meant money. It meant rents. It meant voters in some cases, if he had control over a parliamentary burgh, and it meant prestige. So to build a planned village would be quite a good ploy by the landowner'.

At a time when the opportunities offered by Scotland's cities and towns were a powerful inducement to those who no longer had any hold on the land, the lowland lairds created holding centres in the countryside.

'You wouldn't do it unless you thought you were going to make money. You didn't do it out of pity for the people you were disturbing. But you did it for what was regarded at the time as *Improvement* – that was the big eighteenth-century buzzword,' says Professor Smout. 'An improving landlord would expect to alter the tenure of his estate. He would enclose the fields and what was often called surplus population would move – or be moved – to a little square village where they would do other things than agriculture. Except of course at harvest time; one of the problems of the eighteenth and nineteenth centuries was that you needed far more people at certain times of year than at other times of the year. At hay time and at harvest time you needed the hordes out in the fields to get the crops in as quickly as possible. So people who were weavers, or fishermen, were expected to turn up for work in the fields at critical points of the year.'

It's no accident that of the total number of planned villages built between the beginning of the eighteenth and the middle of the nineteenth century, the vast majority – more than eighty per cent – appeared between 1760 and 1815. This was precisely the time when population increase and the rapid growth in trade led to the consolidation of the lowland farms and the clearances of people from the land.

Although it's impossible to say precisely how many new villages were built – as opposed to those that simply grew around existing settlements – Chris Smout has estimated the number to be at least 130. Others put the figure much higher. Many of these places still exist today, although some have long since evolved into much bigger, and less planned, centres of urban population.

Airdrie, for example, may nowadays be associated with urban, industrial Scotland but it began life as a fermtoun. In 1695 the main landowner in the area, Robert Hamilton, succeeded in getting the settlement designated as a market town and oversaw its early development as a country village housing mainly weavers.

The town's Aitchison Street and High Street were the first to be constructed. By 1795 Airdrie had a population of almost two thousand people and the 'Aul Toon' had been extended to include East High Street, North Bridge Street, Chapel Street, South Bridge Street, Hallcraig Street, Wellwynd, Bell Street (formerly Finnies Lane) and Wilson Street which used to be known as Pump Lane.

Here there was a well which, according to a local poet William McHutcheson, was a source of fun for local children:

I mind when Airdrie Toon was sma'
And me a wee bit wean
Aft wi' a can, a perfect man
I climbed the Auld Pump Lane

When winter cam' and frost was keen
Aft like a railway train
We ladies then at ithers en'
Slade doon the Auld Pump Lane.

By the 1830s, however, coal mining and the subsequent growth in engineering transformed Airdrie from a small rural weaving town into a hotbed of industrial activity. Over the next decade its population rose to more than twelve thousand and by the end of the century it had swollen to nearly twenty thousand.

Planned villages are not just a feature of the Lowlands. Many of the towns along the coastline of Caithness, Sutherland and the Cromarty Firth – among them Thurso and Helmsdale – were built by the local landowners, as were the settlements at Inveraray and the three villages on Islay. In the central Highlands the Duke of Perth built Crieff, the Duke of Gordon constructed Tomintoul, and Sir James Grant founded Grantown-on-Spey.

Many can be found around Moray, Banff and north-west Aberdeenshire; the later settlements, like Hopeman and Burghead which appeared in the early nineteenth century, were fishing communities, but the earlier inland villages, like Keith and Huntly, relied on the linen trade. Huntly – described in the Old Statistical Account of Scotland – was the creation of the Duke of Gordon:

> The village . . . has surprisingly increased within these fifty years, in population and industry, in so much that where all around it for some distance was formerly barren heath, swamps or marsh there is now scarcely one uncultivated spot to be seen; and barley, oats, lint and potatoes, and turnips are produced in abundance where nothing grew before. The spirit of improvement and manufacture was first introduced by a few who dealt in the yarn trade. From their laudable example and from observing the profits arising from industry, others were encouraged; and now it is become one of the first villages of the North . . . Being situated in the midst of a large and fertile country the industrious inhabitants have a ready sale for what they bring to market by which many poor cottagers [cottars] and sub tenants are enabled to pay for their scanty possessions.

Some planned villages were designed to attract industry – places like Balfron, New Lanark and Stanley in Perthshire where the fast-flowing Tay provided the power for a cotton mill. Others like Grangemouth were designed as a port at the eastern end of the Forth-Clyde Canal. In the South-West where the creation of the great cattle ranches had led to clearances and protest in the early part of the eighteenth century landowners were quick to develop existing settlements. Fishing or shipping centres were created at Glencapel and Port William, while the likes of Kirkpatrick and New Langholm relied upon the cotton and wool weaving industries.

The origins of these communities and the way of life led by their inhabitants were diverse, depending as much on where they were as on the improving zeal of their founder. Nevertheless, they all shared a basic pattern of appearance – a 'regularity of structure', as Professor Smout puts it. There was often a simple square or a rectangle of some sort, akin to a village green, around which houses were built. Homes were also strung out neatly along a street with gardens running back. The houses themselves were mainly two or even three storeys high with three, four or five rooms. They were built of stone with tiled or slated roofs.

Unlike many English villages, Scottish settlements rarely had front gardens and a tenant's front door opened directly onto the pavement beside the street. This was a deliberate design feature to prevent householders from placing their midden or dunghill at the front of the house – a common practice in the old fermtouns. The new planned villages were meant to be desirable places in which to live, settlements which would provide a better social and economic framework for the new Scotland which was evolving.

The lengths to which landowners went to ensure this was so are demonstrated in 1735 when one of the earliest improvers, John Cockburn, began to build Ormiston near Edinburgh. The town was laid out on the lines of an English village by a civil engineer from London but he took instructions from the landlord:

> I can give my consent to no houses being built in the Main Street of the town but what are two storeys high. None who thinks justly and wishes well to it can wish to have it disfigured in that particular, or any other that can be prevented. Every man concerned in the place has an interest in having the Main Street appear as handsome and to look as well as we can and not to have little paltry houses . . .

Tenants in the surrounding enclosed fields were encouraged to adopt new farming methods from England and were amongst the first in Scotland to sow turnips in drills and to cultivate their crops in rotation. A distillery and a brewery were also built. Cockburn was eventually forced to sell

Ormiston in 1747 after he overspent, and by the nineteenth century the town's future was dependent on coal mining. That, however, did not stop other lairds from following his example.

Colonel William Fullarton, in his Board of Agriculture Report of 1793, makes it clear that Cockburn heavily influenced the improvements carried out on the Earl of Eglinton's estates in Ayrshire in 1750:

> An eminent farmer Mr Wight of Ormiston was brought from East Lothian to introduce the proper mode of ploughing, levelling ridges, fallowing, drilling, turnip husbandry and rotations of crop. Great attention was bestowed on the breed of horses and cattle. Ploughmen and dairy people were brought from various parts of England. Fences were made on an extensive scale, and the county was beautified by a multitude of clumps, belts, and plantations. The noblemen and gentlemen very zealously concurred in promoting measures so conducive to their own advantage and to the general interest of the country. The demand for cheese and butter to supply the multiplying wants of Glasgow, Paisley, Greenock and Port Glasgow, led to increasing care respecting milch cows and dairies. The English market afforded ready sale for black cattle; and the growing manufactures of the country introduced the benefits of opulence.

The 10th Earl of Eglinton, Alexander, emulated Cockburn still further when he decided to build a planned village on his estate. Inspired, apparently, by a village he had seen during his travels in Italy, he made provision for the new settlement to be laid out on either side of a village green or common area through which the Lynn Burn flowed, the streets converging as they rose up the hill. The green, which was to become known as 'the orry', would be bisected by another street marking out the shape of the letter 'A' – which just happened to be the initial of the Earl's Christian name.

The land was split up and rented out on long leases to tenants – or tacksmen as they were called here who then had to erect their own houses within five years of taking over the lease. They were allowed to quarry stone from the estate and to use stone from the old dwelling houses which were being replaced, but their house had to be built in accordance with strict conditions set down by their landlord. The result was impressive, according to the New Statistical Account of the 1840s:

> two rows of elegantly built houses, all of freestone, with a large space between, laid out in fine green fields, interspersed with trees, with a fine gurgling streamlet running down the middle . . . Towards the higher end, and on a rivulet, the cotton mill stands.

Some of the wealthiest landowners employed distinguished architects to create their villages: Thomas Telford designed Ullapool and Pultneyetown at Wick, William Adam laid out Fochabers and, with his son John, helped build Inveraray. Others initiated schemes which had benefits beyond their own estates. In the Old Statistical Account of the 1790s the Reverend Dr George Lawrie pays ample tribute to the work of John Earl of Loudoun whom he describes as the 'father of agriculture' in this part of the shire:

> He prudently began with making roads through the parish, as early as the year 1733; and an excellent bridge was, by his influence, built over Irvine water; and an excellent road from thence, and from his house to Newmilns, was the first made road in the shire of Ayr, which was done by statute work. He remembered when there was neither cart nor wagon in the parish, but his father's,

> Earl Hugh, and his factor's. Now there are above 250 in the parish, besides wagons for leading grain, peats, &c. Formerly they carried home their grain in sledges or cars, and their coals on small horses. At the same period Earl John began to plant and inclose; he is said to have planted above one million of trees. The trees are mostly ash, elm, oak and many of them are of a great size.

There is little doubt that the landlords behind these projects took enormous pride in their achievements. Their ambitions, in keeping with an age of progress and enlightenment, were often grand – the landowner behind New Leeds in Aberdeenshire clearly had big hopes for his planned village – and these hopes were not restricted to the mere fabric and appearance of the buildings.

Most landlords were on a moral crusade, too. They regarded the unplanned hamlets which were beginning to sprawl across the Scottish countryside and the towns and cities with suspicion. In his Analysis of the Old Statistical Account of Scotland Sir John Sinclair remarked that those living in rural hamlets 'are generally more ignorant, duller and more uncouth than those who are assembled in villages', and in towns 'human nature is liable to temptation, corruption, infirmity of body and a depravity of the mind'. He went on:

> It is from the temperate and healthy family of the country labourer or tradesman and not from the alleys and garrets of a town that the race is to be sought who are best calculated to cultivate our fields or defend our properties from danger . . . villagers are in general contented and unambitious.

The planned villages kept people close to the estate as a handy pool of reserve labour but this was not enough. Professor Smout says that a laird considered improvement not just in an economic or scientific sense; it had a moral dimension as well: 'Improvement has a double sense of improving the output, improving the income of the laird and to be fair to the welfare of everyone on the estate. But it also had a moral meaning, moral improvement. You would improve the character of the local inhabitants'. Under the old system of agriculture they were regarded as idle and indolent. 'That's not surprising,' adds Smout, 'since you didn't have much to do in the winter and you were badly fed; you would expect to lounge about. But both the Church and lairds saw this as a failing among the Scots.'

This soon changed in the towns and villages built by the improving landlords. 'You have visitors to planned villages who praise both the industry of the people and the industry in the economic sense. When Cockburn built the town of Ormiston in East Lothian, one of his friends went round to see the village and he wrote that there were cottages where people were making linen and a little brewery, and "you won't see a child above the age of six at play". So the people became industrious as well as providing industry.'

One of the key aims of these settlements, says Professor Smout, was to keep a working population virtuous and respectful of authority – to create a compromise between the indolence of the old peasant class of farmer and the profligacy of unregulated life in the big towns and cities.

James Robertson, chronicler of agriculture in the county of Perth, observed in 1794 that well-regulated villages where the reins of government had been 'held by a steady hand' produced workers who were steadier, more intelligent 'and certainly more hardy than the deformed spawn and jail-sweepings of the great towns'.

The eighteenth-century landowners could not have been unaware of the social disruption and dislocation their changes caused to many families but they were convinced that as well as being economically vital the changes were also beneficial to the welfare of the people. Many might have been forced from the land, transformed from peasant farmer into day labourer or craftsman, but they now lived in better houses in a more secure and pleasant environment. There was plenty of work to go round, too. There were only occasional periods of unemployment, and in the booming economy sustained by Scotland's transition to industrialisation wage rates for farm labourers rose sharply, by about 250% between the late 1760s and the 1790s.

Little wonder the gentry and supporters of 'the improvements' felt content with the way things were going. James Robertson's *General View of the Agriculture of the Southern Districts of the County of Perth* reflected the general opinion amongst Scottish society's elite:

> No man will venture to say that a farm of fifty acres in the hands of four tenants who have each a horse in the plough and their grounds mixed in runrig will produce the quantity of subsistence which has both money and industry to cultivate the ground. With respect to population, where is the difference whether the other three farmers live on the farm or in an adjoining village? But with respect to industry the difference is great: on the farm they are three-fourths of the year idle; in the villages they are skilful artists and able to rear their families without begging their bread.

According to Chris Smout, one of the main reasons the removal of people from the land in the Lowlands was considered more acceptable than the later Highland Clearances was that those affected were better off as a result: 'If you think about not so much attachment to land as attachment to money, then they were not going to lose. Where there was a big town nearby many of the farm servants left of their own accord because the wages were bigger in the towns.

'For those who remained on the land, or who were evicted from the land and had to depend entirely on waged labour, living maybe in some little cottage with a plot of ground to grow potatoes and a few hens but not much else, all the evidence suggests that they were no worse off than they had been before.'

'Well yes, but Stalin would have said exactly the same when he was collectivising the peasants of the Ukraine,' counters the Highland historian Dr Jim Hunter. 'They were moved to planned villages as well. Clearly being moved to a planned village is one step up from being put on a stinking emigrant ship and transported across the ocean, as many Highlanders were. It wasn't of that sort of scale but it couldn't have been anything other than hugely disruptive and upsetting to many of the people involved.'

Jim Hunter's book *The Making of the Crofting Community* famously chronicled the hardships suffered by those who were cleared from their lands in the Highlands and Islands. He says that while it is possible to argue that many of those who were cleared were better off as a result – whether in the Highlands or the Lowlands – this was an unintended consequence of the process undertaken by the landlords.

He is especially critical of historians who he claims have fallen into the trap of using the language that was used by the landowners and accepting the term 'improvement' uncritically. 'They seem to accept the notion that all this change was for the best in the long run. That's a very dangerous notion to perpetrate because it minimises the horror that was experienced by the people who were on the receiving end of all this.'

In the end it is difficult to escape the conclusion that the landlords' overriding motive for pushing through improvements on their estates and for building planned villages was strictly commercial.

When reading the tributes written by contemporaries to the

great landlords, it is easy to forget that while they may have shown the lead in village construction and the transformation of the countryside, this was not done out of a sense of overwhelming paternalism, still less altruism. These projects were all designed to increase the value of their land and to make money. The lairds were driven by profit. Some may have shown admirable concern for the welfare of their tenants but that did not deter them from raising the rent.

When Alexander, 10th Earl of Eglinton, was shot by a poacher, Mungo Campbell, in 1769 the reaction of his tenants was instructive. According to William Aiton in his Agricultural Report of 1811:

> When Alexander fell by the hands of Mungo Campbell, the general outcry among the lower orders was, that it was a punishment inflicted by heaven on the Earl, for introducing innovations in agriculture, and raising the rents of his lands.

Not that this discouraged his successor. His brother Archibald completed building the planned village of Eaglesham in 1797, at which time the rental value of his land was just over £11,000. Less than twenty years later it had more than doubled to almost £25,000.

Even those held up as 'the epitome of the best eighteenth century improver – astute, careful, farsighted successful and paternalist' were not ignorant of the potential for profit their schemes represented. The Old Statistical Account pays tribute to Joseph Cumine of Auchry in Aberdeenshire for his efforts in helping his tenants:

> Observing that his tenants were frequently at a loss for a market, he determined to establish a permanent one on his own estate. For this purpose, he planned a regular village, contiguous to the church, upon the moorish part

> of a farm which in whole yielded only £11 a year. For a while, he felt in silence the sneers of his neighbours, who reprobated this scheme as wild and impracticable; but these temporary sneers soon gave way to lasting esteem.

Why this change in attitude to Mr Cumine? His neighbouring lairds may well have admired the way he persuaded a few tenants to take up feus, or his generosity in lending money to the industrious or, indeed, his negotiating skills in obtaining premiums for the manufactures. One suspects, however, that what really impressed them was the result of these changes outlined in the same account:

> Settlers annually flocked to Cumines town . . . and the village, built of freestone, soon assumed a flourishing appearance . . . and instead of £11 sterling, the original rent, produce him annually from £120 to £150 a year.

Whatever motive lay behind their construction, the planned villages – and the huge number of unplanned rural settlements which grew up in the countryside – played a crucial role in helping to stem any social discontent caused by the clearances of cottar families in the Lowlands. Despite the unprecedented scale of the social upheaval and dispossession between 1750 and 1830 there was no repeat of the peasants' revolt which greeted the lairds of Galloway when they set about enclosing their lands at the beginning of the eighteenth century.

An inspection of the Old Statistical Account for Scotland reveals that many of the cottars and unsuccessful tenants who were removed from the land during this period transferred to the villages and towns of the countryside.

In places like Fife, Ayrshire and Lanarkshire the records demonstrate that while parish populations rose overall, the country areas were losing people, due to the clearances, and the villages and towns were expanding. In Dalmellington overall parish numbers fell from 739 in 1755 to 681 in 1792. But by this time more than 500, nearly three-quarters of the total parish population, lived within the village. In Stonehouse in Lanarkshire the country population in 1696 stood at 600, and the village was just 272. By 1792 the population in the village had more than doubled to nearly 600 while the number living in the country area of the parish had fallen to just over 450.

Whether they liked it or not – and they certainly had no choice in the matter – the cottars and tenants who lost their hold on the land found alternative employment in these rural villages and towns or further afield in the cities. The booming lowland economy and industrialisation meant few would go hungry.

This was not so in the Highlands. Here the lairds sought to follow the lead of their counterparts in the Lowlands, erecting planned villages and creating crofting communities when they cleared their lands for sheep. But the Highland economy never took off in the way that it did further south – even in areas where it was hoped that the linen industry could thrive.

'One of the problems the Highlands had was that they were an awfully long way from the market,' says Professor Chris Smout. 'So whereas in Angus you could start a little planned village and you are right on the doorstep of Dundee or Forfar and Montrose and there is no problem of disposing of your product, try to do exactly the same thing in Wester Ross and it's almost impossible to get the cloth profitably to market because the transport costs are too much.'

When the fishing and kelp industries foundered in the western Highlands and Islands, there was no alternative employment to be had; the result was an increasingly destitute population. As the pressures of overcrowding and crop failures grew, starvation and death followed.

Thanks to the success of the lowland economy, the fate of

those cleared from the land in the Lowlands was less apocalyptic. But not all who ended up in the villages, towns or cities were happy or successful in their new lives as Scotland's new rural or urban proletariat.

For these people there was another alternative, albeit one which was fraught with uncertainty and danger: emigration.

CHAPTER SIX

Revolution without Protest?

> 'I was put in by the patron, and the people knew nothing whatsoever of me, and their hearts were stirred into strife on the occasion, and they did all that lay within the compass of their power to keep me out, insomuch, that there was obliged to be a guard of soldiers to protect the Presbytery; and it was a thing that made my heart grieve when I heard the drum beating and the fife playing as we were going to the Kirk. The people were really mad and vicious, and flung dirt upon us as we passed, and reviled us all, and held out the finger of scorn at me.'
>
> John Galt, *Annals of the Parish*

The year 1760 began in trying fashion for Rev Micah Balwhidder, newly imposed minister in the parish of Dalmailing as imagined sixty years later by John Galt. Balwhidder was obliged to climb through one of the windows of his Kirk, the rabble having barred the doors in near-riotous fashion. For he was the laird's choice and they had not been consulted. Galt, through the diary of Mr Balwhidder, paints an extraordinary picture of a society in flux from the time of the minister's disputed ordination to his final sermon in 1810. It is the opening scene, however, which suggests a Scotland which was not as much at ease with itself as has often been suggested.

Ministers mattered in the eighteenth century. The Church of Scotland, established in the Reformation of 1560 and enshrined in and protected by the Act of Union in 1707, was at the very heart of local authority. Poor relief, education and social control all flowed from the pulpit to the pews. The doctrine of a Godly people might have been derived from the Highest authority; direction and money came from the social elite. Kirk ministers, who had stood up against kings and lords during the turmoil of seventeenth-century civil wars, were more obsequious in this new 'Age of Enlightenment'.

For the masses, turning up on a Sunday was as much a social occasion as an opportunity to worship. Everybody went to church. It was the one time during the week when people could gather and gossip. For all the talk of God, the religious aspect of the Sabbath may have been something of a sideshow.

Balwhidder's predicament, easing his robust frame through the narrowest of windows against the background of a baying mob, has more than an air of the comical. It may even have seemed so to Galt's readers in 1821. Yet the novelist was also delivering a powerful message which would have been appreciated by his audience. For this was a patronage dispute, something which virtually every one of Scotland's 984 parishes would come to experience between the start of the eighteenth and the end of the nineteenth century.

The Patronage Act of 1712 had restored the right of lay patrons – usually the lairds – to nominate parish ministers. Not only was this a violation of the Treaty of Union, it also flew in the face of Presbyterian precept which gave congregations the right to choose after hearing candidates preach. The removal of this little bit of democracy would eventually have far-reaching consequences. Patronage disputes became a running sore. They were the catalyst which propelled the Kirk towards schism in the Disruption of 1843. Half of the ministers and two-thirds of the elders left to form the Free Church of Scotland. Free from secular interference, they proclaimed their new denomination the genuine, untainted child of the Scottish Reformation.

Patronage disputes may also reveal a deeper malaise in the countryside. They marched across Scotland in the wake of agricultural improvements. From the Borders in the 1740s to Aberdeenshire a century later the power of the lairds was challenged in the only organised way that seemed available to ordinary people. They barred the path of the laird's nominee and cocked a snook at his Kirk. By 1820 one in three lowland Scots had left the national church altogether. The scale of non-conformist worship eclipsed even that of England and might well have been viewed as a challenge to the civil as well as the ecclesiastical establishment.

Was religious trouble popular reaction by proxy to the Agricultural Revolution? Professor Callum Brown of Strathclyde University argues it was. 'The fact that the Presbyterian dissent of Scotland arose at the same time as the agricultural changes and lowland clearances was no accident.' What took place, according to Professor Brown, was a psalm-infested revolution. People used the language of Christianity to express their dissatisfaction not just with what was happening in their parish church but also with what was going on all around them.

This perspective is just one strand of the work which revisionists are now engaged upon. Others, especially Professor Chris Whatley, have looked beyond the landed estates to the towns and cities which burgeoned during the late eighteenth century for evidence of protest which also had its roots in rural Scotland. Theirs is a challenge to the standard view that folk meekly accepted or actively embraced the great changes; that it was a silent revolution.

This argument over just how vocal was the opposition is at the very heart of the debate. Whilst there is virtual agreement amongst historians that the Lowland Clearances happened, that they involved immense upheaval for enormous numbers of people, and were part of the same process which led to the Highland evictions, the big question is how much this rankled. Where is the evidence of significant, concerted, painful unrest?

With the exception of the Galloway Levellers' rising there is no other obvious and major outburst of protest. Across the Irish Sea similar changes brought mini-armies out into the fields to tear down enclosure walls and assert the popular will. South of the Border, attacks on custom and right led to the breaking of threshing machines, culminating in the infamous Captain Swing riots of the early nineteenth century. Yet when William Cobbett, the great English radical, came north, all he saw to his surprise and, perhaps, disappointment was quiescence. It led him to ask why the Scots were not burning the ricks as was the case with his own countrymen? Later still, during the upsurge in demand for parliamentary reform, leading to the great Charter of the 1840s, Scots remained tenaciously attached to 'moral force' rather than 'physical force' to advance their cause. What had happened to the excitable people of the Covenant, to those who took up arms for the Glorious Revolution or to restore the hapless ancient House of Stuart?

Never was the paradox of why the dog did not bark in the night more applicable than when considering the response to the clearances in eighteenth-century lowland Scotland. It is not simply a case of waiting for the revisionists to be proved right. This is an exciting and dynamic field of historiography and much of the work already done comes down firmly on the side of what one academic has labelled 'the orthodoxy of passivity'.

It is almost impossible to measure happiness and beyond the wit of all of us to interview the dead. In the absence of significant conflagration the only way to assess popular acceptance or otherwise is to probe the records of the past; to sift through the sources and interpret the evidence. Again there is agreement that the manner in which people were removed from the land was perfectly legal and therefore, in the main, accepted. There is also a fair degree of unanimity on the power and authority of the lairds. Scotland in 1760 was a rigidly hierarchical country where the lower orders were more used to the firm hand of landlord authority than people living in England or Wales or even Ireland during the same period. Moreover there can be no doubt that the cottars of the Lowlands, unlike the crofters in some parts of the Highlands, had options other than starvation. There had been movement around the countryside even before the improvements began. Folk were, therefore, aware that there was life beyond the land. But here is the judgement call. How much did people acknowledge they were being 'bettered' and how much did they seethe with anger at events that were so obviously beyond their control?

In a comprehensive study of large swathes of lowland Scotland Professor Tom Devine has carefully assessed court records and estate papers. His primary focus was on Lanarkshire where, in the space of forty years, the whole nature of agriculture changed. It is strange to imagine that this area, often regarded as the epitome of twentieth-century urban industrial Scotland, was once at the cutting edge of rural innovation. Improving leases, single tenancies, vastly inflated rents, and the destruction of cottages were the classic hallmarks of clearance. They were exhibited, and proudly at that, throughout the county.

The major landowners retreated from their estates to comfortable residences in London or Edinburgh. They visited only rarely and then positively marvelled at the way their factors had redesigned everything. On the Duke of Hamilton's policies this fell to John Burrell.

He meticulously detailed the processes of improvement which, though they had started in the period immediately after the failure of the 1745 Jacobite Rising, he took forward to a new level. In his journal Hamilton's factor outlined the crops he expected to be planted, the rotations which should be followed, and the rents which would be charged:

> That the tenants within the Baronys of Hamilton, Cambuslang and Dalserf shall be restricted first from ploughing above one third part of their present possessions; second Never to take up ground without lime or some other manure; third Never to take above three crops running; Fourth that all ground shall be richly laid down with clover and rygrass seeds; three good crops of grain and six good crops of grass alternately. Any tenant who acts in a contrary way shall be liable in double rent for the ground otherways cropped.
>
> John Burrell, regulations of his Grace the Duke of Hamilton's estates, 1764.

Under Burrell's stewardship the worth of the land and the harvest it produced soared. He acted with almost total independence, noting the surprise on the countenance of the Duke himself when they took a ride through one particular area in October 1767. His Grace marvelled to see 'corn growing where never anything grew before'. This part of Lanarkshire – under John Burrell – had no need to wait for the stimulus of price hikes which the Napoleonic Wars produced and which prompted many other areas to embrace change. Burrell had been achieving this through judicious management as early as the 1770s. He married new forms of husbandry with 'efficiencies'. The bright were rewarded, the reluctant weeded out. Central to the plan were the enclosure of fields and the engrossment of farms.

It was not achieved without pain. It could not have taken place without significant social upset. Professor Devine found the number of fermtouns on the Hamilton lands fell from thirty-two in the 1750s to eighteen in 1778. Yet Burrell was able to secure an overall acceptance of radical changes from the tenantry and with an apparent absence of trouble from those who could no longer be accommodated on the land.

There is certainly evidence of writs of removal in Hamilton Sheriff Court, but these cannot compare in either number or scope with the legal notices which were served in the Highlands and Islands. Burrell was an improver: he was not thought of as Lanarkshire's Patrick Sellar; there is no record of effigy-burning or attempted murder on this factor. Yet he, too, removed people and introduced sheep.

Nor was the manager of the Duke of Douglas's lands in Renfrewshire and Lanarkshire demonised by the ordinary folk. This in spite of the fact that in the 1770s and 1780s Robert Ainslie presided over a huge fall in population in the parishes of Carmichael, Robertoun and Douglas – the first by thirteen per cent, the second by fifteen per cent and the third by thirty-three per cent.

It might be hard to measure the suffering of those who were removed; it is easier to construct a balance sheet of pounds, shillings and pence which accrued. Rental values in Douglas parish, for example, went up from £980 in 1737 to £2,465 in 1774 and almost £3,000 by the end of the century. Ainslie was not wedded to the notion of big always being beautiful but he was convinced that the old ways were inefficient and tended to encourage indolence:

> In every business which requires money and skill, there must be an object sufficient to attract the attention of the man possessed of these; very small farms present no such object and therefore where they prevail improvements are not to be expected; it is not necessary that every farm should be a large one, a few of them perhaps may be sufficient to introduce improvements into a country.

Professor Devine embarked upon his assessment of the transformation of rural Scotland with an open mind though he readily admits that, given the scope and nature of the improvements, he expected to find widespread evidence of protest; signs of some form of resistance, especially in upland parishes where animals had replaced people – places where the phrase 'Lowland Clearance' sits comfortably. In a telling portion of the interview he gave in the preparation for our radio series, he summed matters up thus: 'We live in a society today where change is a constant. The position in the society we are dealing with is that from time immemorial, usually handed through oral tradition and the knack of working the land, things hadn't actually changed very much. And here we have this enormous upheaval. Tensions must have been increased. There must have been pain because the whole development of this society is towards a market economy – and where a market economy is, there are good times, but there are also bad times with violent fluctuation. We know in 1771/2 and again in 1782/3 there were very difficult times in the lowland countryside, even to the extent where state and landlord intervention had to occur in order to reduce the possibilities of starvation. We are not talking about a pretty world. We are talking about a challenging and difficult time. So one would therefore expect there to be some kind of response. There has to be some kind of protest. Some indications of collective unrest'.

But what he found was . . . nothing. Beyond what he regards as routine vandalism and normal criminality, court records and estate papers revealed only silence. There simply was no incipient revolt in the country. The people worked with and through the changes. It might have been disappointing but the sources could not have been clearer. As to the evidence of the Old Statistical Account of the 1790s, Devine believes caution should be employed. Although many applauded the increase in productivity, others bemoaned the impact on the cottars and the fermtouns which were fast disappearing as a result. However, some of the ministers may have used different terms for the same thing. The overall picture, it could be argued, might be less revealing and more confusing as a result.

This assessment of a tranquil – though far from static – countryside is shared by Professor Christopher Smout. 'What you can say,' he told us, 'is that people in the eighteenth century did not make the same protests about being moved as they did in the Highlands in the nineteenth century.'

Others, though, are less sure. Professor Christopher Whatley, for one, is convinced the protests which ought to have taken place did actually happen. But they have either been ignored, overlooked or categorised as part of something else. The great histories of Scotland came to be written at the end of the nineteenth century when the full horror of the Highland Clearances was still fresh in the public mind, fresh from contemporary reporting, fresh from the starkly painted images which captured the imagination and might even have pricked some Victorian consciences. The contrast of a northern people being led to the emigrant ships with the comfortable cottages and patchwork fields of the Sassenach was a potent one and one vividly captured in the painting by Thomas Faed, 'The Last of the Clan'. Hence highland clearance, lowland improvement.

Professor Whatley has added to the dissection of official documentation by scouring the records for other sources. His picture is of a very different Lowland society, of a late eighteenth-century Scotland which 'is on fire with meal rioting'. The real amount of crime and disorder had been greatly underestimated because much of it never made it to court or was simply not remarked upon in estate papers. To start a case you needed a suspect but if the culprits managed to elude authority, then nothing would be written down. Though some counties began to use a form of police, actual forces didn't emerge until the third decade of the nineteenth century and none was established in Lanarkshire until the 1850s. Those incidents which did make it to official records were by definition the tip of the iceberg. Whatley has concentrated his attention on letters between individuals of rank; on materials such as town council minutes; and on an array of anonymous notes which, he says, dispels the myth of a compliant population:

> As we have been under your tyrannical power so long and been so much keeped under by your old head strong unjust ways of dealing with us about this town. We call you and the Lord Lieutenant two old damn tyrants and robbers . . . you may depend that we will risk ourselves and all that we have before we will pay you nor your constables. If we don't get you on Thursday we will set your house on fire and we will get your old wig and make it dance . . . the whole county and town will assist us in everything.
>
> Anonymous letter sent to William Cunningham of Lainshaw, Deputy Lord Lieutenant, County of Ayr, August 21 1797.

Evidence such as this 'gut-wrenching note' is to be found in abundance, according to Whatley. Historians just need to be a bit more savvy in poking and peeking to uncover the whispered threats and the dangerous glances. It is no great surprise that the revolt in Galloway was not repeated. The shock of what nearly happened in the 1720s delivered a salutary lesson which Scotland's elite never forgot. Landowners were careful not to let similar boils fester let alone erupt.

They pushed through the changes under a cloak of legality. They offered the option of planned villages to those displaced from the land. There was work as day labourers for men like James Somerville or in the mills of the new towns for whole families. In times of extreme hardship it was usual for heritors to buy up stocks of meal and grain and then sell them at cost, or even at a loss, to the luckless peasants. It would be wrong to say this was done solely to prevent trouble. A sense of paternalism was also evident. Equally landowners were motivated by what was in it for them as the commercialisation of the countryside took hold.

It wasn't just the formal alterations to leases or the new regulations on what should and should not be grown which rankled. Lairds could not be challenged over this – their legal rights were universally acknowledged. But that acceptance broke down when estate managers started to interfere with what ordinary lowlanders considered to be their rights.

Even at the best of times cottars and sub-tenants struggled to eke out a living in the runrigs. Central to their continued existence was a bit of paid labour at harvest or during sowing along with their traditional claim to certain customs like the right to graze skeletal beasts on the common land. Or the right to 'glean' – to go into the fields at harvest-time and pick up the odd bit of straw, corn or seed that was lying around. The peasantry were also entitled to enter woods and take away sticks for their fires, to dig peat as fuel or to gather turf to make the walls and roofs of their wattled cottages.

When life was lived on the edge, these were not optional extras; they were central to the family and fermtoun economy. But such practices could not continue when estates were reorganised. Common land, as in the case of the mire of Billie in northern Berwickshire, was assumed and enclosed. Factors wanted the chaff as well as the wheat, and customary rights to glean were regarded as pilfering and all but outlawed by the 1780s. For those who remained on the land, either as tenants or as labouring hinds, these losses were hard to bear. John Home-Robertson, whose Wedderburn ancestors acquired Caribbean plantations as well as a huge swathe of the Merse, says: 'It has been argued that the slaves working on the sugar plantations of Grenada probably had a better standard of living than people working in the farms in Berwickshire'.

The authorities were alive to latent trouble. As James

Robertson outlined in his *General View of the Agriculture of the Southern Districts of the County of Perth*, compiled in 1794:

> It is acknowledged that a watchful eye ought to be kept over villages, no less than all other collections of men; and that the reins of government ought to be held by a steady hand. The superior ought, therefore, to reserve some checks to himself, at least until the community arrives at that degree of intelligence, integrity and power, which will enable it to serve its own prosperity, and regulate its own internal police . . . Weeds will necessarily arise, in an uncultivated field, to injure the valuable part of the crop.

Paradoxically, it was in the urban centres and planned villages, swollen by the rural refugees, that the real impact of lost rights hammered home. Five of the thirteen largest towns in Scotland at least trebled their population between 1750 and 1821. Such unprecedented growth brought with it unanticipated problems. Like Wild West shanty towns these communities regularly outstripped what facilities were available – including the food supply, fuel, and any organised system of law and order. As people concentrated in the slums they compared notes and swapped grievances. It was in the towns that Professor Whatley found the most potent expression of protest.

When work was to be had and wages, however pitiful, were paid, then a lid could be kept on the pot. But when prices rose, for whatever reason, or when mill wheels stopped turning because of business cycles – whatever they were – the new townies were pushed to the edge and beyond. Unable to glean and barred from helping themselves to the huge surpluses flowing out of their erstwhile country homes, they took to the streets. Whatley has charted food riots across Scotland in 1756–7, 1763, 1767, 1771–4, 1778, 1783, 1794–6 and

1800–01. 'What you have here is thousands of people who had previously been able to put together a living in the countryside. In the towns there is the creation of a wage-earning society where people are wholly dependent on their own labour. As wage levels are relatively low that means there's not a lot of slack there.'

The acute food shortages were accentuated in some towns which lay close to the new granaries of, for example, Ayrshire, Angus and the Borders. Vast quantities of meal and grain were being exported while the urban poor starved. It led Professor Whatley to conclude: 'Scotland is on fire with meal rioting because the market system isn't working. It isn't capable of dealing with the harvest failures there were, or if there was a harvest failure south of the Border, you might see Scottish farmers and grain dealers selling there. The consequence of that is a shortage in those very towns through which that grain is being shipped, like Montrose, Dundee, Dumfries, to name but three. These towns are enormously difficult to control in the late eighteenth century. Nothing creates anger as much as seeing a good harvest and not being able, at the same time, to eat'.

There was a strong sense of moral economy in the mob seizing food, mirroring, to a certain extent, events taking place in England. The aristocracy, or at least some of them, were worried. Professor Chris Smout notes the rumour which swept Perth as news of the French Revolution filtered through. 'When you find the Duke of Atholl going into Perth to find people saying 'Off with the head of Citizen Murray' – though it might be a joke – it wouldn't sound much of a joke to the Duke of Atholl considering what was going on in France at the time. There was a great deal of nervousness going on.' Nervousness which is also reflected in some of the letters Chris Whatley unearthed:

> For some time past there has been a great apprehension amongst the inhabitants for fear of a scarcity of provisions . . . The people, thinking everything was to be sent off, threatened to mix all the grain in the Granary to prevent it from being shipped . . . A rumour prevailed that Mr McGlagan was to be burned in effigy . . .
> Robert Cranston to Lord Kinnaird, 28 February 1800.

Fire-raising, effigy-burning, threatening anonymous letters and meal riots. A nation ill at ease with itself, where trouble, stoked and provoked by the inequities of the agricultural improvements, was endemic? Perhaps. And perhaps, given the right spark, the flame of the common man might have burned as brightly in Pittenweem as in Paris. Certainly the authorities were alarmed first with the mushrooming of reform societies across lowland Scotland, then by pro-revolutionary newspaper editorials and finally, and most gravely, by spontaneous rioting along the east coast. Henry Dundas was concerned enough to tell the House of Commons of a mood of serious alarm 'by the great manufacturers, by magistrates and by gentlemen'.

But the spirit of revolution, if such existed, was swiftly quelled by the activities of government spies who infiltrated and doubtless exaggerated the nefarious nature of local societies, and by the widely reported excesses of the 'September Massacres' of 1792 in France. A crackdown on Scottish dissent was not hard to achieve in the aftermath of this wake-up call to the country's ruling classes. Liberty was a fine thing to talk about in the couthy bars of the Old Town; it could not be allowed to spread to the slums of the Cowgate. And spark for the common people there was none. Even allowing for meal riots and the protests fomented against the Militia Act of 1797, Scotland seemed far from the anarchy which consumed Ireland in 1792–4. There were serious incidents like the so-called Battle of Tranent, when soldiers pushed beyond endurance by the taunting of the mob killed twelve people. Other less bloody affairs took place and perhaps their importance has been understated. But it is hard to see any attempted link between the disparate malcontents of urban Scotland.

That judgement is made with the considerable benefit of hindsight and the encyclopaedic researches of a growing band of academics. It would not have seemed quite as clear-cut to the Duke of Atholl and his ilk. Worries over a Caledonian Robespierre emerging to lead the masses must have been serious, especially in the wake of decades of deference. Class differences were supplanting feudal hierarchies but sometimes the insolence of the lower orders seemed to know no bounds.

In the days before Culloden landowners across Scotland had judicial supremacy in their own fiefdoms. Their allies in the Kirk provided the back-up of spiritual authority and often assisted in ferocious demonstrations of magnate power – the most obvious examples being the witch-hunts which scarred much of lowland Scotland for a century or more from the late sixteenth century. These were less to do with concerns over satanic practices and more about the re-establishment of control by the elite over a restless population.

Such blatant and naked power over life and death had gone – at least in the rural Lowlands by the mid-eighteenth century. It could not endure the great changes or the gradual evolution of class structure. But the link between laird and minister remained and was firmly secured by the Patronage Act of 1712. Other departures from the normal Presbyterian form of service followed. Fixed pews were installed, replacing the stools which worshippers had always brought from home. These were then rented. People had to pay. Certain areas were reserved for the better-off, and this found its apogee in what became known as 'lairds' lofts' – upper-storey chambers which provided privacy and discretion. No need any more to even meet or rub shoulders with the locals. Folk might have had a favourite spot in the Kirk, but now they were almost given a designated space. A bit here for the factor, another part for the farm stewards, yet another area for the tenants, and over there, at the back, the farm servants and peasants. The lay-out of Lowland society was given almost physical representation on the floor of some Presbyterian churches.

Psalm books pushed out precentors who had once taken their place at the front of the Kirk to 'read the line' of each hymn and who still exist to this day in many churches in the Western Isles. For landowners intent on improving mores and morals, as well as earth and industry, such a practice reeked of embarrassing parochialism. To many individuals, and to some entire congregations, tampering with traditions their forefathers had died to protect was much too much to thole. Secession churches sprang up and dissenters vented their anger very publicly in patronage riots and in more subtle Sabbath ways. John Ramsay, a nineteenth-century Perthshire landowner, lamented the growth of new groups like the Antiburghers – dissenters who were more vigorous in their objections to the rule of the gentry:

> Not many years ago, in walking upon the highroad, every bonnet and hat was lifted to the gentry whom the people met. It was an unmeaning expression of respect. The first who would not bow the knee to Baal were the Antiburghers when going to Church on Sunday. No such thing now takes place, Sunday or Saturday, among our rustics, even when they are acquainted with gentlemen. It is connected with the spirit of the times.

That spirit of the times was a fracturing of respect. Professor Callum Brown, the pre-eminent expert in the field, notes the importance of the 'walk' to church. It could take many hours to get from home to Kirk on the Sabbath. As the eighteenth century drew to a close, this activity almost became an expression of an individual's right and grievance. It became 'a day when their ethos of suffering, particularly at the hands of the landlords who were evicting others, was recalled'. Caps were no longer doffed and the people would not bow or scrape. 'The Scottish Sabbath changed from being a day purely of rest and worship of God into a day of protest even, perhaps arguably, into a day of class struggle.'

This was the most obvious and perhaps the only way most Scots, especially in the countryside, would have felt able to show their discontent. Parliament was distant and did not interfere with their daily lives. Fewer than two-and-a-half thousand men had the vote in any case. Real power resided in the shires with the landowner and a minister who was often his placeman. The sea change in a society which now allowed for vocal or physical opposition to a minister and the snubbing of the laird should not be dismissed lightly. In the 1690s witches were burned in Berwickshire after commissions of lords and clerics so decided. People were made to watch as their friends or family members were torched to melting soap. Fifty years later the grandchildren of those who were cowed into watching the torture would not even cross the street to give the landowner the time of day. Deference, whilst far from being dead, had been breached. It increased the nervousness of the aristocracy at times of crisis, especially when the monarchy fell in France.

Healthy historical debate is now taking place over whether or not Scotland was on the cusp of a real revolution as the agricultural one raced ahead in the mid- to late eighteenth century. This was a period of remarkable and rapid change. It would be more than surprising were there no evidence of serious upset in some parts of the country. But the new system of land management and the start of the industrial age needed people. It is a great irony that, at least in the beginning, neither was particularly technological. For the countryside to bloom and for the factories to operate, labour, and lots of it, was essential. In spite of the periodic upsets in the towns, living standards rose with each decade. The same was true for those who remained on the land. Wage rates for farm labourers increased by about 250% between the late 1760s and the 1790s. These statistics, however, have to be tempered with the realisation that the base level from which the increases came was very low and that even in good years families still spent on average two-thirds of all they earned on basic foodstuffs.

Perhaps the fairest assessment of whether Scotland was settled or agitated is to be found in the much-maligned Scots law verdict of Not Proven. There is plenty of evidence of protest, but is there a pattern? Religious dissent threads through the age and almost seems geographically to follow improvement. But does that confirm an unsettled country? Scotland does explode with with a big idea in the eighteenth century. It altered the landscape and the social structure forever and did so at lightning speed. The foundations were undoubtedly laid for the delivery of a more productive country which would provide greater opportunities and sometimes even affluence. Yet did this immediately make people happier and more content? Did they look back to a Golden Age of affinity with the soil; or did they retain a folk-memory of the times when death came at the age of thirty-five and starvation was a regular feature of an altogether miserable existence? If this new Scotland was so fantastic, then why were so many thousands pushed or pulled away to foreign lands?

The jury is out.

CHAPTER SEVEN

Emigration – the dripping tap

> Erected on behalf of Arran clearance descendants across North America to their brave forefathers who departed from their beloved island home to Canada during the clearance years 1829 to 1840. Here at Lamlash on April 25th 1829 part of the clearance (86 souls) when embarking on the brig Caledonia (196 tons) the Rev A Mackay preached from the mound (opposite) formed by the departing. His text 'Casting all your care upon him; for he careth for you.' (1st Peter ch.5 v.7.)
> The Caledonia arrived at Quebec City June 25 1829. The group was the first of more than 300 Arran colonists of Megantic County, province of Quebec. The largest group, more than 400, had as their destination the seaport town of Dalhousie, New Brunswick to be pioneer settlers of the Restigouche Bay Chaleur District.
>
> Yet still the blood is strong, the heart is highland.
> A chlann eilean mo ghaoil bithibh dilease d'a cheile.
>
> Memorial to the Arran Clearances
> unveiled by Mrs Myrtle Cook Maxwell
> of New Brunswick, Canada 9 May 1977

Yet still the blood is strong, the heart is highland. Emigration would not change that fact of life for those cleared from the straths and glens. For those whom clan ties could not protect. For those who would stay close as kith and kin in a foreign land. But is Arran, an island in the Firth of Clyde opposite the Ayrshire links, really part of the Gaeltachd? Lamlash Bay, where the unfortunate Arranites departed for Canada, is geographically further south than Berwick-upon-Tweed. Crofting legislation, passed in the 1880s, was never extended to the island or its people.

Without minimising the trauma of what took place on the Duke of Hamilton's estates in 1829, perhaps the Arran experience is more Lowland than Highland. It is clearance nonetheless.

The Hamilton policies on mainland Scotland had been rigorously improved almost from the moment news filtered through of the crushing of the Jacobite Rising in 1746. But the momentum did not come from Hamilton Palace, the family's ancestral home. The Dukes gave almost total freedom of action to their managers – and especially to John Burrell who, as factor, comprehensively changed the nature of the landlord-tenant relationship in Lanarkshire from the 1760s.

Thousands of people were obliged to leave their traditional runrig holdings and many fermtouns were thrown down to make way for large, commercial units. The lucky ones who managed to keep a foothold on the land still fretted about the possibility of being obliged to leave at the end of their nineteen-year lease. Perhaps they would fail to satisfy all of the 'improving' clauses. Or perhaps they had worked too hard and had bettered the land to such an extent that it was now ready to be slotted together with other small farms to further consolidate, modernise and rationalise. It was all legal, so what was the point of protest? In any case there was the option of working for other tenants or employment in some of the new mill towns which were springing up on the fringes of the fields. For those who could not endure the discipline of the factory and the rent book there was always emigration. The one option denied them was that of remaining as tenants on the soil.

The reality of what happened in eighteenth- and early nineteenth-century Lanarkshire echoes down to the events that took place on Arran in 1829. The differences may help shed some light on why the Lowland experience of clearance and emigration has remained shadowy until now.

The ducal estates on Arran were exposed to change from the early 1770s. John Burrell tried to apply the same principles there as he was using in Lanarkshire. But the process was piecemeal and lacked proper direction. It was not until 1815 that wholesale improvement was driven through with a vengeance. Such action, according to the agricultural writer William Aiton, was long overdue:

> It is the fault of the proprietor alone that those [tenants] on Arran have not become as intelligent, industrious and liberal as people in their rank on the other side of the firth. They and their forefathers have been always kept, and to this day they are uniformly placed in a situation that debars all improvement on the soil and on their own condition, intellectual or pecuniary. When any of the inhabitants of Arran are placed in advantageous circumstances in any other quarter, they are as active and intelligent as those of any other county: and if the proprietors of land in the neighbouring counties of Ayr and Renfrew etc., had managed their estates till now in the way that that of Arran has been conducted, the inhabitants would have been to this day as ignorant, indolent and prejudiced as those of Arran.
> William Aiton, *General View of the Agriculture of the county of Bute*, 1816.

In the twenty years after this bruising commentary was delivered, improvement fully took hold on Arran. The new methods were pursued with rigour and with firmness. The outcome has a familiar ring. Farms were united and multiple tenancies put to an end. Tiny holdings of just a few acres could barely sustain a family, let alone provide a decent amount of rent. Those tenants who lost out were absorbed into what industry Arran could offer – either as labourers or fishermen – or struck out westwards to Ayrshire a mere fourteen miles away. As was the case on the mainland, tenants on Arran first railed against the changes and then came to accept and adopt them.

Those who kept their farms were given written leases – leases that had expiry dates. In 1829 every one of these agreements for the Glen Sannox portion of the island ran out. It was then that the Duke's factor decided that sheep would be a better bet than people in the hilly terrain of the glen. At a single stroke twenty-seven families were told to leave.

It is this suddenness and the simultaneous collective fate of a community that mark the Arran experience out from that of the cottar families who were similarly thrown off Hamilton land in Lanarkshire. It is the suddenness that makes the Sannox clearance a classically Highland one. That and the fact that the peasants spoke Gaelic.

They could have sailed to the mainland in search of work or tried to scratch a living from the sea in one of the coastal villages on the island. Some did. But around half immediately opted instead for the challenge and opportunities of Canada. This again confirms the Sannox exodus as one of clearance. Twelve families, comprising eighty-six people, were not just quitting the land, they were quitting old Scotia. As they trudged up the boards of the brig *Caledonia* which berthed in Lamlash Bay on Saturday 25th April 1829, a Church of Scotland minister intoned from the Bible:

> Cast all your anxiety on him because he cares for you. Be self-controlled and alert. Your enemy the devil prowls around like a roaring lion looking for someone to devour. Resist him, standing firm in the faith, because you know that your brothers throughout the world are undergoing the same kind of sufferings. And the God of all grace, who called you to his eternal glory in Christ, after you have suffered a little while, will himself restore you and make you strong, firm and steadfast. To him be the power for ever and ever. Amen. 1st Peter ch.5 v.7 11.

You can almost taste the salt from the sea mixing with the tears of the bereft now leaving Arran forever – names including McKillop, Kelso, McMillan, McKinnon, McKenzie, Brodie, Cook, Hendry and Stewart.

Others would have left but there was no room on the brig which was already more than half-full when it departed Greenock en route to its stop-off point in the Firth of Clyde. In all, 180 people crowded the little ship as it cast rope for the ocean. There is no record of where the other ninety-four hailed from but it is possible that at least some of those seeking a new life abroad were once tenant farmers who, like the Sannox folk, had failed to be granted an extension to their lease. Perhaps one or two, or more, were victims of Hamilton's factor on the Lanarkshire estates.

The passengers aboard *Caledonia* each paid £4 a head. Except that the Arranites did not. The Duke provided half of the cost of the voyage for the islanders – and when they arrived at Quebec on June 25th 1829 the twelve families from Sannox could each look forward to a 100-acre plot eventually secured at Megantic County, Quebec. This again was provided by the efforts and influence of the Duke of Hamilton.

Cleared they had been. But who on the *Caledonia* had the

better prospects as the brig steered towards the wide and unforgiving Atlantic – those from Sannox or the other emigrants who had to provide for their own passage and who had little but hope awaiting them in Canada? Contemporaries had nothing to say for the latter group but plenty of sympathy for the Arran folk and more especially at the manner of their removal. The author James Hogg contributed this to *Blackwood's Magazine* eight months after the *Caledonia* left Scotland:

> Ah! Wae's me, I hear the Duke of Hamilton's cottars are a' gaun away, man and mither's son, frae the Isle o' Arran. Pity on us! Was there a bonnier sicht in the warld, than to sail by yon green shores on a bonny summer's evening, and see the smoke risin' frae the puir bodies' bit shielings.

There is little now to show where people once lived in Glen Sannox. But the same is true at Lour in Peeblesshire and at the site of hundreds of other lowland settlements where, to use Hogg's description of Arran, the *cottars are a' gaun away* as well.

It has been estimated that 75,000 people left Scotland between 1700 and 1780 – at least 60,000 of these came from the Lowlands. They were the shock-troops for much more substantial emigration in the nineteenth and twentieth centuries, providing familial and community links with the old country. Dr Marjory Harper of Aberdeen University has calculated that two million Scots departed for North America, South Africa, Australia and New Zealand between 1800 and 1911, and though perhaps as many as a third returned home, this still represents a huge slice of Scotland's population. Dr Harper's work shows the exodus was by no means Highland-dominated. On the contrary it was predominantly a Lowland one: 'The analogy I like to use is of the flood and the dripping tap. I think one reason that we focus so much on Highland emigration is that it was dramatic, and it happened in short, sharp bursts if you like. I think even that is maybe erroneous because in many parts of the Highlands there's also the dripping tap analogy, particularly from the Eastern Highlands. From Easter Ross and the east side of Inverness-shire. But the dripping tap makes the bath overflow in just the same way as the flood does. What was happening in many parts of the rural Lowlands was the constantly dripping tap of depopulation that was going on right throughout the nineteenth century, and before that century and throughout that century and beyond. We don't notice it so much because sometimes people didn't emigrate straight away. Sometimes they went to towns first of all. But even if they emigrated straight away they were not going in large swathes, as was the case on many highland estates and which was commented upon by many external commentators'.

In recent years letters, diaries and journals have been uncovered which add flesh to the statistical bones of the great Scottish diaspora: stories of pain and regret as well as of hope and opportunity from Lowland farmers who had lost their land usually in the same way as the tenants of Glen Sannox – by the legal expedient of notice to quit on expiry of a written lease. John Beech, another specialist in North American emigration, discovered this letter from Margaret Stevenson of Kilmacolm in Renfrewshire to her son Robert who had moved to St Andrews, New Brunswick. She talks of her other son John – who had left home for Prince Edward Island – of the movement of many other families from the Kilmacolm area, and the reasons for their departure:

> Robert Orr, Hardridge, and James Arthur from Hurton went to Prince Edward Island with their families in 1820. Your brother went in the same vessel. Along with

him there went Alexander Laird, Burnbank, and family; James Laird, Nutton, and family; James Houston, Woodend, and family; James Sample, Mount Blow, and family; Alexander Lang Jr., Botherickfield, with his wife, newly married; George Nisbet and family. The old woman went along with them, 105 persons in all. The vessel stopped a short time at the Island and returned bringing the greatest number of letters to Kilmalcolm that ever came from a foreign land either before or since, being little short of a hundred . . . We can get a letter from John once a year. He has got up a house and a loom and has as much work as he can do himself. The boys manage the farm. His daughter is married. We had a letter June last. They have been all in health since going there. Their cattle have thriven well. Crops, and all, equal expectation.

The lawsuit respecting the Ducal estate was settled in May 1821. The following list includes all the farms from which tenants have gone or have been turned out since 1818: 1, Burnbrae; 2, Midbranches; 3, Burntbank; 4, Greenside; 5, Lukerton; 6, Tounfoot; 7, High nutton; 8, Laighwood-head; 9, High Hugh; 10, Laigh Hugh; 11, Hardridge; 12, Horswand; 13, Burnbank; 14, Midtoun; 15, Bridge-end; 16, West Lawpark. There are six more sequestered upon the estate.

Margaret Anderson Stevenson, 10th March 1823.

Evidence of clearance or improvement? There is no cairn to mark the Renfrewshire evictions nor, as far as we know, any society in Canada which remembers those who left in large numbers to find a new life and help found a new country. How many were 'turned out' in the manner of those listed from the above 1821 lawsuit, and how many quit voluntarily? It is impossible to say. Scots had a long tradition of seeking betterment furth of their own shores. From medieval Poland to the seventeenth-century plantation of Ulster; from the disaster of Darien to the riches of a British Empire built on Caledonian canniness. Scots on the move and Scots on the make was nothing new.

In the eighteenth century emigration societies flourished in the Lowlands. The best known, according to Dr Harper, was the Scots American Company of Farmers, formed by 138 individuals at Inchinnan in Renfrewshire in 1773. Helped by Rev. Dr John Witherspoon, formerly of Paisley and then later a prominent signatory of the American Declaration of Independence, the Inchinnan farmers purchased a large chunk of modern-day Vermont. From north and south of the Highland Line others likewise made their way to the quays at Greenock, Port Glasgow, Aberdeen and Leith. There was an obvious attraction: 'Land in abundance, land which they could buy; land which they could buy for an equivalent of a year's rent at home and land which would be theirs in perpetuity without interfering landlords, tithes and taxes,' says Dr Harper.

The Inchinnan pioneers might well have been joined by the most famous eighteenth-century farming family in Scotland. The Burns family had struggled on improving leases in Ayrshire, spending twelve miserable years at Mount Oliphant. When he was still a boy Robert was forced to do a man's work, clearing the fields of stone and ploughing the sodden clay ground. It contributed to the ill-health which brought death at the premature age of 37 but it also inspired some of the most powerful verses ever written. The dignity of labour, as described in the *Cottar's Saturday Night;* equality of existence, as shown in *A Man's a Man;* and the inequality endured by the honest toilers of the earth, as voiced in *The Twa Dogs:*

I noticed on our Lords court day
An mony a time my hearts been wae
Poor tenant bodies scant o cash
How they man thole a factor's snash
He'll stamp and threaten, curse and swear
He'll apprehend them, poind their gear;
While they maun staun wi aspect humble,
An hear it a' and fear and tremble.

Burns scholar Gavin Sprott told us: 'What Burns is referring to in fact is personal experience. Because after the former owner sold Mount Oliphant the new laird was not as easy going. And Burns had a personal memory of just what he described of the laird or his factor demanding a rent. And really putting the screws on. And people so obviously upset and harried and harassed and in tears. And Burns never, ever forgot that'.

Had it not been for Robert diverting the profits of the Edinburgh edition to his brother Gilbert, the farm and the family might well have been totally sunk. Like many others, they had already given consideration to life in America.

Lowland emigration has usually been portrayed as a movement of the willing. But were the people who took that course, having lost their lease or having been thrown out of work in an economic downturn, 'pulled' by that opportunity or 'pushed' into that option? Dr Harper has noted that 'for poverty and to get bread' was the reason given by the 212 passengers who shipped from Greenock to New York in February 1774. Most were Paisley weavers made destitute by unemployment.

Three months later the 62 who sailed on the *Gale* from Whitehaven to New York cited 'want of employment' and 'racked rents'. These accounts were doubtless the tip of the iceberg. They also underline one other defining feature of Lowland, as opposed to Highland, emigration. Though some went straight from the fields, the bulk of them had first tried to make a life in other ways in the mills, as weavers, as labourers. To add to Dr Harper's metaphor of the dripping tap and the flood, the great Highland movement happened in a few dramatic leaps while Lowland emigration first took a hop, skip and a jump through the towns.

Emigration societies, letters from friends and family and the activities of colonial agents all helped smooth the road to the quayside. At times of crises, such as the 1820s when handloom weaving collapsed, emigration was a virtual mania. So many wanted to quit Scotland that the ships couldn't keep pace with demand and lots were often drawn by those anxious to quit Scotland. By the 1840s Paisley, the weaving capital of Britain, was so depressed that a special parliamentary investigation took place. It led to the reform of the Scots Poor Law but that was hardly likely to have put the brake on would-be migrants hiking to the coast. They left in search of land and the American (or Canadian or Australasian) dream. Land, though no longer as plentiful as it had once been, was still there to be had. The dream of riches and ease, though it remained a fantasy for most, became the reality for a few.

George Craig's family had once been cottars in Berwickshire. Cleared from the land when improvements kicked in, they moved to the village of Coldingham and became linen weavers. In the 1790s when the Old Statistical Account was compiled, life was apparently good for that trade in that small bit of Scotland:

> There are about thirty-six weavers in this parish who, besides what they weave for the inhabitants, manufacture a good deal of linen and woolen clothes for sale. They are generally in easy circumstances, and some of them are becoming rich in that line of life.
>
> Old Statistical Account, Parish of Coldingham, County of Berwick 1794.

This proved to be merely a transient interlude between the drudgery of the fields and the cold reality of capitalism. Within a few years the new factories had swamped the market with cheap, mass-produced cloth. Outworking was dead and these former aristocrats of labour were thrown on to the poor roll. With no future at home, George Craig quit Scotland in 1827 at the age of 18. Arriving at Quebec with nothing but a knapsack, he quickly got a job and earned enough money to pay for the passage of his entire family.

Shortly afterwards the Craigs moved to New York and prospered. George's brother Peter made a fortune in the Gold Rush of 1849 and his son John founded a shipyard on the Great Lakes. As late as the 1890s John Craig was calling on his Berwickshire cousins to move to the land that had delivered far more than Scotland ever could. Eventually the family, wealthy and now wholly American, switched their interests to Long Beach, California.

George Craig arrived in Quebec two years before the *Caledonia* carrying the Arran settlers pitched up at the very same port. Like other Lowlanders he had no land secured and awaiting him but there is little doubt that he would have been every bit as apprehensive about his future. For Craig, as for the Sannox folk, the old country was now in the past. He was no farmer and there was no Berwickshire corner of Canada to gravitate towards, so Craig felt comfortable about moving around in this vast new continent. His experience is typical of the Lowland migrant. Though some, especially those from rural areas, did forge their own communities, these lacked the cohesion of Gaelic enclaves. The majority of Lowlanders who left came from Scotland's towns and cities. Farming was an option but was just one of many potential avenues of employment. Those who have studied emigration say Lowlanders, much more so than Highland Scots, were able to integrate and assimilate with whatever new society they found themselves in.

The Sannox people, by contrast, knew they were joining kin when they arrived in Canada. The original Arran settlers there were not those cleared in 1829. Others had gone of their own accord to Bay Chaleur in New Brunswick from the 1770s.

Highlanders generally found a little part of home waiting for them after the rough Atlantic crossing. United by a distinct language and a shared culture, they were much more likely to stick together, and the stories they shared have been handed down so that the full horror of the clearance experience has remained a constant. They also wrote home often to encourage family and friends to follow them. William Henry sent word to his mother on Arran in 1834 that a small colony of migrants had established themselves in Quebec. In Arran Gaelic he told her that life was better in Canada though sometimes he yearned for home:

> My dear cousin Uillean Ruadh is well; he is sometimes employed as a carpenter and works the land the rest of the time, and he has some hopes that the rest of his family will come out, but he does not know, and I can well believe that they would be better here than where they are and many other people besides.

The first Arran settlers moved to North America at the same time as other Highlanders were also voluntarily quitting their ancient homelands. Dragged along by the same 'pull' as peasants from across Scotland, tacksmen, or superior tenants, organised ships to take the willing. It was a movement that caused no little upset to landowners. Late eighteenth-century emigration was not considered a good thing by the chieftains. To some it was a matter of tradition and paternalism; but to most it was because on unimproved estates people were a precious, economic commodity.

The topography and climate of much of the Highlands were ill-suited to the improved crop rotation and agricultural practices being introduced elsewhere in the country. Instead of consolidating their territory, landlords took the opposite course and fragmented their lands. Holdings were divided and then divided again, creating the crofting townships that many assume were there from time immemorial. In order to survive on such scanty acreage, clansmen took on other work primarily as seaweed gatherers and kelp manufacturers on the coast. It was backbreaking, soul-destroying, poorly paid labour. But it sustained huge numbers of people on otherwise marginal land and it drew incredible wealth to the now often absentee, and most certainly distant, chieftains. Such was the fear of losing the people on whom this new wealth depended that Westminster responded to landowner pleas and passed the 1803 Passenger Act – a misnomer if ever there was one. The thrust behind this legislation was to make emigration all but impossible – as was outlined by the bill's author Charles Hope:

> I had the chief hand in preparing and carrying thro' parliament an Act which was professedly calculated merely to regulate the equipment and victualling of ships carrying passengers to America, but which certainly was intended . . . indirectly to prevent the effects of that pernicious spirit of discontent against their own country, and rage for emigrating to America. Quoted in James Hunter's *The Making of the Crofting Community*.

Denied the safety valve of free movement, the population on some Highland estates soared above the ridiculous. Whilst kelping was buoyant, it was in the interests of the chiefs to maintain as large a pool of labour as possible. But when, in the years after 1815, the collapse in that industry began to hit home, people became a problem. Prices for prime kelp declined by two-thirds between 1823 and 1828. Kelp went from being lucrative to marginal. At the same time cattle prices fell, which was another sorry blow to the heart of the crofting economy. The population of whole regions of the Highlands and Islands were pushed to the brink of subsistence. Then in 1846 came the disaster of potato blight. Around seventy per cent of parishes in the north and west reported the total ruin of the crop. The aching pains of hunger, a familiar part of a crofting family's existence, were replaced by starvation and famine.

The number of people who died in the Highland Famine has never been accurately established. It didn't rival the number of those who perished in Ireland in similar circumstances in the previous year, and by the summer of 1847 death rates in most parts had returned to normal. But the famine which subsequently seared the consciousness of Scotland and still provokes such strong feelings today was also a catalyst for the resumption of emigration on a most active scale. Landowners took the initiative to rid their estates of populations that were no longer tenable and helped fund the passage of up to 20,000 Highlanders to Canada in the late 1840s. Here, truly, was the flood being siphoned into emigrant ships which carried at least part of a nation in their holds.

Initially public opinion, as directed by certain newspapers and journals, applauded. Much of the language was overtly racist. The Gaels were a sub-species, morally and intellectually inferior to the Saxon. This appeared in the *Scotsman* in July 1851. It demonstrates just how far Scotland had travelled from the eighteenth-century consensus of one nation, one people:

> Burdensome and useless . . . Collective emigration is, therefore, the removal of a diseased and damaged part of our population. It is a relief to the rest of the population to be rid of this part.

As the flood continued, the fate of those left was scarcely improved. Highland landowners now shifted their estate strategy away from subdividing their holdings to the creation of large single units.These farms, in the main, were not arable but stock-based. Crops were hard to grow in the poor soil and hilly landscape but sheep were ideally suited to the terrain. Professor Tom Devine summed things up thus: 'In the Highlands the trajectory of landlord policy moves to two extremes. It moves first of all to fragmentation and then to consolidation. It is out of that interaction that the real horror of the Highland Clearances takes place'. The lands of those who left were not shared out amongst those who remained. They were annexed to the new sheep farms.

Professor Smout has calculated that there was an eleven per cent fall in the population of the Highlands in the forty years after 1851 – when clearances were most pronounced – yet an eighteen per cent decline in the rest of the country. Of the eleven counties that reached their historic peak in the mid-nineteenth century, four are in the Lowlands. There was no potato famine to force starvation on the poor of Kinross, Berwickshire, Kirkcudbright and Wigtownshire, but still people left in droves. It is entirely probable that the majority ended up much more prosperous and content than they would have done at home. It may well be the case that lowland Scotland is more productive and settled as a result. That has been the accepted wisdom. But north or south, Highland or Lowland, how did those people who left feel as Scotland disappeared forever over the horizon?

The modern world is a small one. Affordable supersonic airline travel and frequent foreign holidays have given those of us from the west a rich perspective on other lands and other cultures. But how many of us would be comfortable about moving abroad for good – even if that seemed to offer a better lifestyle, a more secure future for our children, an easier path to old age? It is still a very daunting prospect. How much more daunting, then, it must have been for our great-great-great grandparents when they stepped down on to the bare boards of flimsy-rigged luggers that tossed ominously even in the calm of harbour?

For two million Scots during the nineteenth century that was the reality they chose or the path they were pushed towards. Whether forced out in a moment by factors bearing flaming torches and supported by police and sheriff's officers; or told to quit at the end of a given term of tenancy; or barred from the gates of a factory which had closed down; or having chosen the risk of something better, Scotland was no longer to be their home.

Australasia, Canada, America, New Zealand, South Africa. Lands of chance and lands of opportunity. Lands where no masters, either Lowland lord or Highland chief, would call the tune. John Stevenson, who had struck out from Kilmacolm for Prince Edward Island in 1820, sent the following poem home to his mother. It is no haunting Gaelic lament for the past days and the clan. Instead it is a call to leave Scotland and improve, not someone else's fields, but Lowlanders' own lives:

> We here do not need weapons
> For warfare that are made,
> No, nor scaling ladders
> To climb the balustrade
>
> Till we arise like heroes
> Our purpose to pursue
> And show the brave Canadians
> How Scottish boys can plow.

Emigration

All you who are in hardship
And cannot pay your rents,
You need not fear to venture
Your lot along with us.

The soil is dry and fertile,
We have a verdant sky,
And all that land produceth
It can be sold quite high.

Our belly is our factor,
He may us crave severe,
But if we should run in arrears,
He will not poind our gear.

When he sends us a summons
It costs us no expense,
And with sequestrations
He never threatens us.

Those who some years before us
Have from oppression fled,
An ocean of difficulties
I find they had to cross.

But now they roll in plenty,
Their barns with wealth are filled,
And cattle in abundance,
They have upon the field.

Those lines for to conclude anew
We bid you all adieu,
We mean not to advise you
But tell you just what's true.

We mean not to deceive you,
From no sinister view
Your coming or your staying
To us no good can do.

John Stevenson, Prince
Edward Island, c.1820

CHAPTER EIGHT

The Rural Refugees – one family's story

> 'From the point of view of ordinary people in Scotland it was not so much improvement as disruption of a lifestyle that generation after generation had known. Working on the land, on their own small plots of land, was something they had been doing for centuries and, all of a sudden, to have no connection to the land must have been a pretty traumatic shock.'
>
> Bruce McCowan, Scarborough,
> Canada, February 2003

Bruce McCowan orders us to slow down. He jabs a finger towards the snow-covered cliffs above Lake Ontario. 'This is the original settlement of the McCowans over a hundred and sixty years ago,' he says. 'They settled right at the edge of the lake because it was pretty much the only small location where they could find land to farm.'

We are driving through Scarborough, one of the wealthiest districts on the outskirts of Toronto, and Bruce is guiding us around an area peppered with million-dollar homes and long gardens stretching down to the lakeside cliffs, known locally as the Bluffs.

Bruce and his relatives are the reason we have come to Canada. As we admire the broad multi-lane highways, the spacious parks and the slender tower blocks of the Toronto skyline it's hard to appreciate that in the early nineteenth century this was frontier country – a wild and untamed wilderness where thousands of Scots, cleared from their Lowland farms, came to settle. Among the refugees from Scotland, exiled by the Agricultural Revolution, was Bruce's ancestor, James McCowan.

James McCowan arrived in Canada in 1833 with his wife Margaret Porteous and their eight children. They made the journey by ship from Greenock, disembarking first in Quebec and then continuing up the St Lawrence River to Toronto – a settlement then known rather unflatteringly as Muddy York.

It was a journey undertaken by thousands of Lowland Scots during the period of the Agricultural Revolution. The McCowans were accompanied by a number of other families from their native Lanarkshire and they were joining many more who had already made the trip. One of them was John Torrance, a land surveyor, who's credited with founding the Lanarkshire settlement in Scarborough. It was he who rented the land at the Bluffs to the McCowans when they first arrived – but it was hardly a prime farming plot.

'This piece of land would have been occupied only by enormous white pine and sturdy oak trees,' says Bruce. 'They'd have been two hundred years old even then and what this land meant was a lot of hard work. The family had to clear the land of trees but once the trees were cut that was really just the beginning; they still had to remove the stumps and that was an enormous task, too.'

But it was work the McCowans were more than willing to undertake. They had re-established their hold on the land and could, with luck, look forward to the prospect of moving up from working someone else's land to farming their own.

'It was a start,' explains Bruce. 'What brought them to Canada was the promise of owning land themselves. The reason they came was to have their own land – a means of sustaining the family without being dependent on the whims or needs of the landowner. They had their own wants and needs and that's what they wanted to achieve without the external influences around them, disrupting the family fortune.'

Back home in Lesmahagow James McCowan had good reason to distrust the 'external influences' around him. His career as an industrialist evaporated amid the money-market nervousness and depression which followed the end of the Napoleonic Wars, while his efforts to return to farming, initially successful, were ultimately thwarted by the improving ambitions of a new landlord.

The McCowan family originally came from Ayrshire. James's father, Robert, lived with his family in several parts of Cumnock before being moved off the land. By the end of the eighteenth century they had turned to coalmining for a livelihood, working at Lord Dumfries's Garlaff Coal Works.

Coalmining was a highly competitive business and many of the colliers were mere serfs. Laws passed by the Scottish parliament in the seventeenth century had made them, and their families, little more than the property of the coal master. Their wages, however, could be relatively good and far higher than anything agricultural labourers could earn. According to contemporary records at Garlaff, mine workers received an annual wage of about £20. The going rate for farm servants in the area was just £7–10 a year.

There is no documentation to confirm it, but it seems that James McCowan was a collier serf who in 1799, following emancipation, bought a lease to run his own coal works. In the spirit of the age this 26-year-old collier was convinced his entrepreneurial endeavours in the new capitalist world would soon make him a man of means.

A small upland farm in Lanarkshire in the relatively underdeveloped Douglas/Coalburn coalfield, some twenty miles from Cumnock, caught his eye. It had six coal seams, ample supplies of limestone, for fertilising the soil, and plenty of ironstone for supplying the emerging smelting industry in Scotland.

When he took over the East Auchanbeg coal works, James also took on the farm which went with it, signing long leases from the owner of the Stockbriggs Estate, James Corbett. James McCowan was now the coal master, employing at least five families, and he was optimistic about the future.

He immediately began to plant trees and lay out gardens around East Auchanbeg farmhouse. The improvement of the grounds was a sign to all of the coal master's position and standing in the community. The full extent of James's ambition and his faith in the ways of the free market is, perhaps, revealed in the decision, in 1813, to rename the property 'Clattering Hall'.

Within four years, however, James McCowan was in financial difficulties. Labour and operating costs during a time of increasing worker unrest, contributions to the capital cost of installing a steam-powered engine at the mine works and the burden of helping to supply housing for the colliers drove up his debts. In 1817 he was outbid for the renewal of the lease of the Auchanbeg works and, although he continued in the business further north at Blackwood, he was finding it impossible to repay the money he owed.

Eventually, in desperation, he turned for help to his brother David who had been living in Trinidad since his own emancipation from the Garlaff mine. But James was to be disappointed by the letter he received on July 1st 1820:

> Dear Brother
> I received yours of the 18th September & 10th April. I am very sorry to see you have been so badly in your health and so oppressed with creditors. Your request of £150 should be complied with it if it was in my power but, believe me, you are misinformed of my ability . . . if it was in my power at this moment I would send you not only the £150 to get clear of your creditors but £150 more to take you to America for I think Britain is going fast to ruin . . . I hope you will not think it is want of inclination that I do not assist you at this time as if you knew my

situation for some time it is not much better than your own.

I remain Dear brother your affectional brother, D McCowan

David, it appears, was also having money difficulties and could offer his brother little but sympathy.

James McCowan was not the only one struggling to make a go of things in Lanarkshire in the second decade of the nineteenth century. The Scottish economy was by now in full recession, and across Scotland many were suffering real hardship and poverty.

Those originally displaced from the land who had not melted away to the factories in Glasgow and Paisley had turned their hand to weaving, and by the early 1800s this was the mainstay of rural industry. In Lesmahagow parish the population rose by almost 50% during the first decade of the century as a result of the expansion of the weaving economy. Now people had fallen on hard times.

Things were little better for the farmers and agricultural workers. The hill country of much of Lanarkshire was less fertile than other areas and farming improvements were slow to catch on. Crop yields were low, the market was depressed, and poor weather added to the sense of crisis. The *Clydesdale Journal*, a newspaper based in Hamilton, reported:

> The weather has been through the spring quarter, as during last winter, mild and wet to a very uncommon degree We had rain more or less almost every day through the month of April. People became so anxious during the last two weeks of that month, that many began to sow whenever the sun was unclouded for a few hours at a time. But to this day, the ground has never been in anything approaching a proper condition for receiving the seed; some have sown without harrowing;

> others have hoed in the seed; some have thrown in the seed between the horses and harrows; while others have gone the round of duty, by sowing and harrowing through thick and thin; leaving the rest to chance.

The combination of poor weather and the depression meant that landlords received lower rents and were forced to offer abatements. An agricultural observer reporting to the Duke of Hamilton Estate in 1817 wrote:

> Matters are looking no better here since you left us. The weather has been mostly wet and very unfavourable for ripening the crops, which are very late. I have been over the baronies of Lesmahagow, Avondale and Shotts last week and . . . I am really persuaded that the prospect at present is no better than last year. In this case, you may lay your account with difficulties. Indeed I do not see how the rent can be got from a number of tenants.

Accounts from the various agricultural fairs in Ayrshire, Dumfriesshire and Lanark reveal that farm labourers and servants were also finding employment difficult to come by and wages were low.

The parlous state of the economy was making survival almost impossible for all but the wealthiest. In her book *Adventurers and Exiles* Marjory Harper estimates that by the winter of 1819 around 15,000 people in the West of Scotland, especially in the counties of Lanarkshire and Renfrewshire, were dependent on charity. An indication of the seriousness of their plight is given in this account in Hansard of the remarks made by the Lanarkshire Whig MP and landowner, Lord Archibald Hamilton, in the House of Commons:

> Many persons in that country [Glasgow] were in such an absolute state of destitution that they looked on their existence as a burthen which they could scarcely support.

> They could neither maintain themselves nor their families; and the period was fast approaching, when without food and without raiment, they must either perish, or prolong their existence by the plunder of their neighbours . . . He [Lord Hamilton] must say, that, from the spirit and temper of ministers, they seemed to have under-rated the distress which at present existed in the northern part of the kingdom.

The government was coming under growing pressure to help people move abroad; emigration was increasingly being regarded by the ruling elite as a form of poor relief. Landowners in the West of Scotland were instrumental in persuading the government to help pay for the cost of the transportation. According to research by Dr Harper, those who took up the offer of assisted passage could expect a loan of £10 from the government, to be repaid within ten years, free transport from Quebec to their final destination in Upper Canada, a one-hundred acre grant and free allocations of seed corn and tools.

Emigration societies mushroomed in the western lowlands, and in January 1819 the people of Lesmahagow organised petitions seeking assisted passage. In May the following year the *Clydesdale Journal* published this notice:

> Emigration to Canada: Several Emigrant Societies in and about Glasgow, and a Society in Lesmahagow, having applied to the County of Lanark for aid and facilities to obtain settlements in the British Colonies in North America, their case was submitted to His Majesty's Ministers . . . An extensive emigration is not contemplated this season; but it is probable a numerous body of people will apply to government to get out on similar terms next spring.

As he struggled to meet his debts, it is unlikely that James McCowan was unaware of this opportunity, and when, in 1821, his coal and limestone business was sequestrated he must have been tempted.

Instead he chose to stay, returning to the occupation which had sustained his ancestors: farming. He no longer leased the coal works at East Auchanbeg but he retained the farm and for the next ten years tried to made a living from breeding cattle and growing crops. Here too, however, 'external influences' were to frustrate him.

Like almost all of the farms in the area, East Auchanbeg was not very productive. Its 146 acres were organised along the lines of the 'old agriculture'. It was divided into an infield or croftland, an outfield, meadows, braes and pasture. At least some of the rent was still paid 'in kind'. According to the leases, tenants on the Stockbriggs estate were required variously to give the landlord 'several hens @ 1/6d' or 'two days work of two horses and carts'. Those who leased larger holdings were expected to contribute towards the minister's stipend, the schoolmaster's salary or the poor funds. They also had to pay part of the cost of building the roads.

There were signs at the beginning of the nineteenth century that the owner, James Corbett, was preparing to modernise his estate and introduce the new farming disciplines already established elsewhere, but he died before the work began. His death ushered in years of litigation over the ownership of Stockbriggs, and there were further legal disputes as creditors of the new co-owners sought to gain control of the income the estate produced.

Through it all a judicial factor, appointed by the courts, ran the estate and made available a proportion of its income to the tenants to undertake limited improvements. In spite of the legal wrangles this was a period of relative stability for the tenants who had guaranteed tenure until the late 1820s when their leases would all expire together.

In 1828, however, Stockbriggs was sold to a new owner, John Gibson, the procurator fiscal in Lanark. As the public prosecutor in the Sheriff Court he was a highly educated man well versed in the law and, more significantly for the tenants of his new estate, more than acquainted with the measures needed to make way for improved farming techniques.

The improvements which had transformed the countryside elsewhere had been slow to come to this part of Lanarkshire but John Gibson was determined to change that. Almost seventy years after the first major lowland clearances of the agricultural revolution began, Auchanbeg and the other farms on the Stockbriggs estate were about to feel its unsettling effects.

Within weeks of taking over, John Gibson produced new leases for his tenants outlining, in writing and in impressive detail, exactly what was expected of them. They contained precisely the kind of provisions used by estate owners in other parts of the Lowlands, emphasising the need for frequent liming and fertilising of the soil with dung, the importance of weed control and the construction of fences and enclosures. The articles of lease would run for nineteen years:

> The tenant to preserve all the Planting from injury by his cattle . . . Landlord to have power to make additional fences which the tenant is bound to keep in repair. Reserving game with liberty of hunting and fishing to Landlord and friends. The tenant to reside on and stock the farm according to the best rules of husbandry, and not to deteriorate the same, never to have less than two-thirds of the arable ground of said farm in grass properly sown down with a sufficient quantity of perennial rye grass and clover seed, along with the first crop after

> fallow potatoes or turnips sufficiently manured, never to take two whole crops running particularly at the expiry of the lease two-thirds of the land shall be left in grass.
>
> Five pounds in additional rent to be paid for each acre cultivated in contravention of the foregoing and to be considered not penal but pactional.
>
> The tenant to cut all docks, ragweeds, thistles and other noxious weeds at the proper season before the seed ripens . . . the tenant to keep and leave fences and houses in repair at the end of the lease. The tenant to consume the whole fodder upon the ground and lay the whole dung annually upon the lands.

The new leases placed the relationship between tenant and laird on a strictly business footing – there was little notion of paternalism evident in the precise legal phrases outlined in the new documents:

> If two years rent is suffered to run in arrear the Lease in the option of the Landlord shall become void and null without power in the tenant to purge the irritancy after an act of removing shall have been raised against him.

The real problem for James McCowan was the cost of the new lease for Auchanbegg. Laird Gibson wanted more than £70 a year in rent – nearly five times the amount James, and other tenants, were used to paying for their farms. Contemporary documents indicate that James, at least, was more than aware that this was far more than he could afford. In his formal offer to accept the Gibson lease he attempted to negotiate:

> I James McCowan farmer at Auchanbegg hereby Offer the yearly rent of seventy-three pounds ten shillings Sterling for the farm at Auchanbegg partly possessed by me being Number Second on the plans of the Estate of Stockbriggs, and consisting of one hundred and forty-six

> acres Imperial measure or thereby . . . but deducting thirty three pounds ten shillings yearly for the first seven years of the Lease and twenty three pounds ten shillings for the next seven years of the Lease and upon the terms and conditions contained upon the ten preceding pages . . .

It was a bold but futile move. Within two years of signing the formal lease at the full £73–10–00 demanded by Gibson he was once again in financial difficulties. He still owed money from his previous occupation as a coal master and by 1831 he was falling behind in his rent. For the McCowans it was the end. They were bankrupt and the landlord went to court to have their belongings and farming tools seized.

From the legal documents narrating the sequestration process it's clear the family were left with very little. The Sheriff Officers – legal officers responsible for carrying out the orders of the court – drew up an inventory of the items to be poinded, or impounded, and then auctioned off. They included 'whole corns, cattle, household furniture and other effects . . . Viz seven cowes . . . five calfes, one horse, one Sow, sixty sheep, four Mug Pettes [a breed of sheep], three Corn Stacks one cart with cart harness . . . one harrow, one plough, one churn and stalf, one eight day clock and case'. Mahogany drawers, desks, chairs, mirrors, fire irons and bedding were also taken.

The McCowans were not the only ones to suffer. During John Gibson's time as laird of Stockbriggs at least five other farms changed hands: five other tenant families driven from the land by the advent of the new capitalism and the free market forces unleashed during the agricultural and industrial revolutions. 'They are all being effectively forced from the land,' says Bruce McCowan. 'They really don't have much choice at this point. They cannot afford to pay five times the rent that they had been accustomed to paying up until just a few years earlier. They've got to the point where something dramatic has to happen.'

In 1833 Bruce's ancestor, James, decided he had no option but to leave his native Scotland. By now there was no chance of any help from the government – assisted passage from the Lowlands was a thing of the past but at least the foreign shores of Canada offered the hope of something better and, with luck, the family could resume their farming ambitions.

Luck, however, was not a commodity lavished upon James McCowan. Having settled in Scarborough, the McCowan family – James, his wife Margaret and eight children ranging in age from three to nineteen – set about preparing their rented plot of ground for cultivation. On August 20th 1834, just over a year after arriving in Canada, James wrote to a relative in Scotland with bad news:

> We have in the course of God's providence lost one of our familie. Our dear daughter Mary Ann Hunter McCowan is no more. She departed this life on Saturday morning the 26th of July of typhus fever and Elizabeth and Jean have both had it but thank God they are both better but Willm is just now very ill of cholera and wither he will get better or not is known to God only . . . This letter I have penned sittin at my son Willms bedhead . . . the cholera is again very sore. God grant that we may all escape it . . . Mrs McCowan is not well and has lain the most part of this day, what the consequences will be God only knows, may it be favourable for us all is my humble wish and prayer. I hope you will excuse bad write and also bad dite for I am so confused and worried that I hardly know what I do not having got much rest for three days and two nights. I am Dear Sir your sincair old friend with I hope a new face, James McCowan.

Eight days later James and another of his children, David, were also dead – victims of the cholera epidemic which had gripped the Scarborough district. It was left to James's surviving sons and daughters to build the new life the family was seeking.

They became active members of the early Scarborough community, building on the work of the early pioneers who were chiefly, though not exclusively, Scots who came from the Eskdale area of Dumfriesshire and from Lesmahagow, Strathaven and the neighbouring parishes in Lanarkshire. The graveyard of St Andrew's, the oldest church in Scarborough established by the Scots community, pays silent tribute to the families who worked so hard to make a new life in this part of Canada: the Bowes, Brownlies, Clellands, Dicksons, Flemings, Muirs and Stobbs; the Pattons, Pattersons, Purdies and Weirs; and the Thomsons, Torrances, Wilsons and Youngs. All of them came from lowland areas of Scotland.

The experiences of those early pioneers and their struggles to establish themselves on the shores of Lake Ontario have been handed down through generations of the McCowans and their relatives. Helen Annis McCowan says: 'I'm always very proud of the fact that all my forefathers came from Scotland on both sides, and my mother's people, too'. Her husband's ancestors, the Thomsons, came from Dumfries. 'We have no idea the hardships they must have had. The first David Thomson who came out, he built a cabin out in Scarborough, and he would walk back to Muddy York, to Toronto, to work as a stone mason. And he did have land out in Scarborough and eventually farmed and most of his sons farmed.

'His wife had several children and I think the first woman she ever met after she lived out there for a while was an Indian woman, and there would be wild animals coming around the doors – bears and the like – because it was right out in the woods. It was really difficult for her but she survived and raised her children.'

For all of the early Scots in Scarborough life must have seemed like an unrelenting battle for survival but most prospered – including James McCowan's surviving sons and daughters. For a while his three sons stayed on at the original 35 acres they had rented from John Torrance. They spent years clearing and farming the Scarborough Bluffs in an area they called 'the flats'. By 1846, however, records in Canada show that the two eldest sons, Robert and James Whiteford McCowan, were still tenant-farmers but they had moved on to work other, larger plots in Scarborough. His youngest son, William Porteous, was the last to leave the original farm but the first to become a landowner, purchasing a plot in the north-east of the town in 1848.

According to the 1861 census, William, his mother and youngest sister, a housekeeper and a hired hand all shared the log cabin he built there – a house which has been reconstructed and now stands as a museum in Scarborough's Thomson Memorial Park. He also purchased other lands in the town, securing a 60-acre farm in the south in 1869 and two plots in the west in 1894. William never married but when he died he passed on his farms to his three nephews and was wealthy enough to pay his former housekeeper a $60-a-year annuity for the rest of her life. William's brothers also eventually moved into ownership. James Whiteford bought a plot in March 1855 and Robert bought 125 acres in 1876.

For the man who has traced the family history, Bruce McCowan, this was a significant moment: 'Owning land was something that had been a foreign concept to them in Scotland. The potential for owning land in Scotland was practically nil but the connection with the land was crucial. They had been on the land for several hundred years; they had been tenant-farmers, they had been coal masters, and to have land taken away from them must have been a real disastrous event.

'The McCowans, the previous generation, had been cleared from the land in Lowland Scotland and I think their value system largely developed on the basis of what the earlier generations had gone through. They gained a respect for being connected with the land. They gained a great respect for knowing that the land could provide, and I think the individualism that was born out of the Agricultural Revolution actually helped them develop the value system that made them successful in Canada; I think they got a sense of individualism that they could not get out of the prevailing social and economic structure in Scotland.

'Emigration to Canada and the promise of owning your own property, the promise of being landowners, was what really drew them here. It's been good for James McCowan's descendants for sure. Robert became owner of about 300 acres and altogether the three McCowan brothers owned about 800 acres in Scarborough', he adds.

Within twenty years of arriving in their adopted country the McCowan brothers had succeeded in realising James's aspiration: they were now a family of major landowners, people of property independent of the 'external influences' which had so blighted their father's fortunes in his native land on the other side of the Atlantic Ocean.

CHAPTER NINE

Conclusion – the Scottish Clearances

> 'Yet it is a fact that morally and intellectually they [Highlanders] are an inferior race to the Lowland Saxon – and that before they can in a civilised age be put in condition to provide for themselves and not to be throwing themselves on the charity of the hard-working Lowlander, the race must be improved by a Lowland inter-mixture; their habits, which did well enough in a former stage of society, must be broken up by force of Lowland example . . .'
>
> James Bruce, journalist,
> *The Scotsman*, 10th February 1847

By the mid-nineteenth century the agricultural revolution had transformed Scotland's lowland countryside. The majority of individual estates were now models of farming efficiency and innovation. Landlords, by and large, prospered as did some of their favoured tenants. Now it was time for the improvers to bring the 'liberating' influences of the free market to land management in the Highlands and Islands.

For those who had seen the 'benefits' of improvement in the Lowlands the traditional ways of Highland farmers, their Celtic customs and Gaelic language were regarded as backward and uncivilised. The sentiments expressed by James Bruce in the *Scotsman* were not uncommon amongst Britain's ruling elite.

Much is still made of the racist abuse which the Scottish establishment heaped on the Gael in the nineteenth century prior to and during the clearances in the Highlands and Islands. Yet this attitude of contempt mirrors similar comments made about the cottars and sub-tenants a little over half a century earlier by those forging ahead with the changes in the Lowlands. William Fullarton in his Board of Agriculture Report on the County of Ayr refers to the 'deep-rooted prejudices against innovation' displayed by the ordinary people who 'were ignorant and indolent'. Other commentators spoke disparagingly of those who preferred the old ways and who opposed the improvements as 'an encroachment on the liberties of the people' and who regarded the farming changes as tending only to 'augment their labour'.

The Agricultural Revolution created two Scotlands: in the Lowlands the consolidation of farms and the introduction of the new practices have entered history as an outstanding success; but in the Highlands and Islands the same policies have left a legacy of poverty, injustice and anti-landlordism which endures to this day.

But in both areas thousands of people were removed from the land, cleared to make way for sheep, cattle or regimented fields of commercially viable crops. In both areas there were evictions and terrible suffering and in both areas whole communities were shipped abroad in waves of emigration. Why, then, is it that these traumas live on so vividly in the traditions of the Highland community but in the Lowlands there seems to have been no significant impact on the collective psyche?

For Dr Jim Hunter the answer is straightforward: 'I think what really differentiated the Highland Clearances from clearances in the Lowlands was the speed and the brutality in the Highland case. The processes involved were similar. It was the same sort of change in agrarian structure and agricultural practices. But whereas in the Lowlands it took years or decades, in the case of England hundreds of years, by the time you reach the north of Scotland it was being done in a matter of weeks. And so when Patrick Sellar cleared the straths of Kildonan and Strathnaver, he cleared dozens of townships in a few days. That concentrated destruction and the brutality involved – that sudden eradication of township and villages – there was nothing anywhere in the Lowlands that in any way compared to that'.

While this is undoubtedly the case – no-one can credibly deny the traumatic reality of the Highland Clearances – at least part of the answer also lies in the differing contours of the land itself. 'One of the great weaknesses in traditional historiography in Scotland was to divide the two societies,' says Professor Tom Devine. 'Landlordism, the market influence, population increase, ideology, all the forces that made for the agricultural revolution in the Lowlands were operating also in the highlands.

'For a number of reasons the changes worked in the Lowlands – usually to do with things like climate; the fact that much of the agriculture in the Lowlands was labour-intensive arable agriculture and it was surrounded by areas of industrialisation where there were alternative opportunities for labour. Whereas in the western Highlands and Islands industrialisation did not take off so the alternatives were weak. Plus the lie of the land meant that many parts of that territory were best fitted for capital-intensive pastoral farming. If you wanted to see it in shorthand terms: the processes were identically governed by similar forces, but the outcomes were quite different.'

If history has paid less attention to the clearances in the Lowlands, then this is due in no small part to the language used in describing the process of agricultural change. The very terms 'clearance' and 'improvement' are highly loaded and subjective. As Professor Chris Smout observes: 'If you use the word 'improvement' you are seeing it very much from the viewpoint of the laird who assumes that what he does ultimately will be for the good of everybody and this is of course not the case. When you talk about clearance you imply a kind of total ruthlessness by the Highland lairds who had no humanity and simply swept people aside in terms of profit. That again is oversimplifying it because it overlooks the problems the Highland lairds had of how you are going to accommodate these people on your estates without going bankrupt yourself'.

He adds: 'I think a fair balance must admit the degree of social disruption – of clearance – in the Lowlands but also say in the Highlands there were genuine efforts to improve the lot of the people'.

It isn't just a question of terminology, however. You don't have to travel very far to come across physical evidence of the clearances in the Highlands and Islands. Anyone who's ventured beyond the tourist tracks on places like the Isle of Skye cannot have missed the moss-covered remains of long deserted cottages and sheilings. These stone remnants are the physical reminders of what happed to whole communities exiled from the glens and straths. In the almost identical landscape of upland Lanarkshire, the South-West and the Borders the monuments to clearance are few and far between. Some, like Lour in Peeblesshire and Glenochar close to the M74 near Abington, still exist but most have disappeared.

The evidence of the Lowland Clearances, however, can still be found in abundance. How else could a Canadian, thousands of miles across the Atlantic Ocean, produce so much fascinating material about such a crucial period in Scotland's past? Bruce McCowan has doggedly tracked down the fortunes of his forebears who were forced from the land one hundred and seventy years ago. 'There are volumes and volumes, box-fulls of documents that are quite relevant from the family point of view – the Court of Session papers, the parochial registers, estate papers, Court of Session records as they were summarised in printed format. There are masses of supporting information to back up the fact that the Lowland Clearances actually did happen and did happen in a very dramatic way, ' he says.

It's hard to escape the conclusion that with a little more application and perseverance countless other family stories are waiting to be uncovered. Here is where the real history of the Lowland Clearances is waiting to be told and that is what sustains academics like emigration specialist John Beech: 'It's important to know because it gives a balance to Scottish history. A lot more people were affected by lowland clearance than by highland clearance but not everyone appreciates this because the Highland Clearances are such an emotive subject'.

He goes on: 'More people left the lowlands of Scotland than left the highlands of Scotland throughout the eighteenth and nineteenth centuries. There was a gradual haemorrhaging of people from the Lowlands. It wasn't like the mass migration from the Highlands – it wasn't so obvious. Plus the fact that people in the Lowlands didn't have a spokesperson. They didn't have a body like the Highland Society of Scotland lobbying for them'.

One of the reasons why there are still crofters in the Highlands but no cottars in the Lowlands is that by the late nineteenth century political lobbying on behalf of the suffering populations of the north and west ensured government intervention. Late it may have been and imperfect it undoubtedly was, but the resulting legislation gave crofters security of tenure – something the cottars and sub-tenants of the Lowlands never enjoyed.

'In the 1880s in the western Highlands and in places like Skye, the Highland Land League was very much on the go and there was unrest, agitation and rent strikes and so on. Having first tried to repress this – at one point they sent the army to Skye to restore order – the government eventually conceded the crofters' demands and crofters in 1886 got security of tenure so they could no longer be evicted,' says highland historian, Jim Hunter.

But the new law didn't apply to all areas where small-scale

farming still survived. 'There was a Royal Commission of Inquiry which travelled around and took a lot of evidence and actually the final verdict was that the law would apply only to those counties which this commission visited. It was no more scientific than that. But there were pressures, obviously from the Scottish landed establishment of the day, that if this was to be conceded at all, the areas to which it applied should be kept as small as possible.'

The crofting legislation did not extend any further south than Argyll and Inverness-shire. Aberdeenshire, Moray, Perthshire and the island of Arran all remained beyond the scope of the act – even though, at that time, small-scale farming was the principal source of husbandry in these areas. Had the act applied to the whole of Scotland, then it's more than likely that the vast arable farms we see today in the North-East would never have come into being.

'These people got a raw deal,' says Dr Hunter, 'and, in fact, in Arran right to this present day there are, in a sense, people who are crofters but who are without the benefit of the protection of the Crofting Acts. That's been a source of some contention in Arran right up to the present time.'

The suffering of the crofters in the Highlands and Islands in the nineteenth century still has the power to prick the political conscience of a nation in the twenty-first century. Much of the early work of the devolved parliament in Edinburgh has been devoted to bringing land reform legislation onto the statute books and was seen by many MSPs as a means to right the wrongs of the past.

But the clearances were not unique to the Highlands; they were a Scottish phenomenon, and the forces which drove them forward have helped to shape our entire country. Labour MSP and Berwickshire landowner John Home Robertson says that what happened in the eighteenth century – the enclosures, the improvements, the creation of big farms in place of the common grazing system – completely altered the landscape of Scotland: 'The more efficient food production allowed the population to increase and added to the wealth and the prosperity of the nation of Scotland and the United Kingdom'.

It is still assumed by most historians that however disruptive the results for individuals and families, the process of improvement was ultimately good for Scotland and for rural society. But for some like Dr Hunter this is a debatable point.

'If you look at the areas that were devoted to large-scale sheep farming – whether in the Highlands or in the Borders – you find empty deserted glens where there is not a new house from one end of the glen to the other; where there are very few people living, where economic prospects are poor and where the surviving agriculture is being kept going solely by vast, enormous subsidies from Europe,' he says. 'If you go, by contrast, to the unimproved parts of Scotland, if you go to the crofting counties, if you go to an island like Skye, for example – where you see the sort of agriculture that so many historians imply was backward and of no great consequence and was better removed from the scene – then you see a much more viable society.

'If you go for instance to the Sleat peninsula of Skye you will see a landscape that is awash with new houses; where all sorts of opportunities have been created; where people are moving in in large numbers and where the population is rising; where you have a vibrant rural society of a kind that simply doesn't exist for most of the rural Borders.

'I think the people who resisted the improvements and condemned them have had the last laugh. I think the unimproved landscape of the crofting counties is a far better one, a far more sensible one, a far more economically viable one today than the big farming landscape peopled by a few subsidy junkies that you get in so much of rural Scotland where improvement was given full reign.'

Dr Hunter's views may be considered startling, even controversial. But controversy and the issue of the Clearances have seldom been strangers. Those few who try to deny them provoke thunderous condemnation and indignation across Scotland, and the memory of the injustices suffered in the crofting communities has bred an almost universal suspicion of modern landowners – especially in the Highlands where the unquestioning loyalty of the people was betrayed by the clan chiefs as they emulated their Lowland counterparts in clearing their estates.

It's worth remembering, however, that the onset of commercial pressures resulting from population growth and free-market capitalism did not discriminate between social classes. While it's true that most of those whose lives were disrupted were the peasant farmers – those who had little legal protection – these were unsettling times for all.

Bruce McCowan's ancestor, James, was forced off his land in Lanarkshire when he could no longer afford to pay the rent. A new landlord, John Gibson, a lawyer, had demanded five times more for the improving leases on the farm at Auchanbegg as he set about trying to make the Stockbriggs estate more profitable. But wealth and learning during the time of the Agricultural Revolution were no guarantee of success, and a year after he left for Canada James McCowan received a letter from a friend suggesting that laird Gibson may also have been in financial difficulties:

> I see Stockbriggs going about in Lanark today. He has advertised, or rather the person from whom he has borrowed the money, has advertised Stockbriggs for sale. I believe he is altogether dependant on what his wife can squeeze out of her Father for his maintenance. The report is that he wants to go into some small farm which at present is let to Sandilands, & reports say he has offered

him £200 to give up his tack [if] he should get hold of the money.

That landowners, too, could feel the cold draught of the downside of the free market is not a fact readily acknowledged by many in the contemporary debate over land management in Scotland. It is true, nonetheless, and the fact that the agricultural and industrial revolutions produced such a dramatic transformation so quickly has left its mark on Scots' attitudes to society and change.

Professor Chris Smout observes: 'There was tremendous suffering and problems and resentment as well as tremendous amounts of money made. It was a very contested and riven thing in Scotland, the industrial and the agricultural revolutions. This made the Scots, particularly in the twentieth century when the bottom fell out of Clydeside in the interwar years and after the Second World War, very suspicious of economic change. You see very conservative trades unionists and you see the employers themselves sort of hesitant. You don't get the feeling in Scotland, until quite recently, that it was a country that embraced change with enthusiasm'.

'To understand this is part of the understanding of how we came to be the way we are as modern Scots,' says Professor Tom Devine. 'It's very important in terms of probing what is distinctive about the Scottish historical process. Scotland was at the very edge of economic development with England but fortunately, from a historian's point of view, the Scottish process was much more rapid. It was a classic industrial and agricultural revolution. It's almost a case study of modern development from a subsistence or peasant-based society to a modern urban and industrial society, and that story has a relevance to developing countries today.'

In countries like India we see rural populations moved out of their villages to make way for hydro-electric schemes, and in

China we see millions displaced as the Yangtse River is dammed. However these events are portrayed, the trauma for those affected – often people without a voice or legal protection – is immense. These, too, are clearances in the name of progress and improvement; they are just as much a part of the twenty-first century as they are features of eighteenth- and nineteenth-century Scotland.

Select Bibliography

Recordings and Interviews

This book is based on a series of three programmes broadcast on BBC Radio Scotland in May/June 2003 under the general title of *The Lowland Clearances*.

Programme One: One Scotland. Transmitted on Sunday 25 May 2003
Programme Two: Winners and Losers. Transmitted on Sunday 1 June 2003
Programme Three: Highland Improvement, Lowland Clearance. Transmitted on Sunday 8 June 2003.

Lengthy interviews were conducted with the following academics and specialists in Scotland:

Professor T. M. Devine, Director of the Research Institute for Irish and Scottish Studies, University of Aberdeen
Professor T.C. Smout, Historiographer Royal for Scotland and Emeritus Professor of Scottish History at the University of St Andrews
Professor Christopher Whatley, Dean of the Faculty of Arts and Social Sciences, University of Dundee
Professor Callum Brown, Department of History, University of Strathclyde
Dr James Hunter, Chairman of Highlands and Islands Enterprise
Dr Marjory Harper, Department of History, University of Aberdeen
Ed Archer
John Beech, European Ethnological Research Centre, National Musuems of Scotland
John Home-Robertson MSP
Alastair Livingstone
Gavin Sprott, National Museums of Scotland

Interviews with the following were also conducted in Canada:

Bruce McCowan, The James McCowan Memorial Social History Society (www.mccowan.org)
George Edward McCowan

Nancy McCowan
Peter McCowan
Robert McCowan
Margaret Lawrie
Helen Thompson
Shirley Scott
Shirley Jarvis

Unpublished and Original Sources

Home of Wedderburn Mss (National Archives of Scotland, GD/267)

Lough, James, The noblest work of God: Autobiography of a Working Man (unpublished diary, 1929. Historical Collection of the Great Lakes, University of Bowling Green, Ohio, United States)

Articles

Brown, Callum, 'Religion and Social Change', in Devine, T. M. and Mitchison, Rosalind (eds.), *People and Society in Scotland, Volume 1, 1760–1830* (Edinburgh, 1988)

Brown, Callum, 'Protest in the Pews. Interpreting Presbyterianism and Society in Fracture during the Scottish Economic Revolution', in Devine, T.M. (ed.), *Conflict and Stability in Scottish Society, 1700–1850* (Edinburgh, 1990)

'Burns' Ayrshire as portrayed by his Contemporaries', in *Ayrshire at the Time of Burns* (Kilmarnock, 1959)

Devine, T.M., 'Scottish Society, 1760–1830', in Devine, T. M. and Mitchison, Rosalind (eds.), *People and Society in Scotland, Volume 1, 1760–1830* (Edinburgh, 1988)

Dunbar J.G. and Hay G.D., 'Excavations at Lour, Stobo 1959–60', in *Proceedings of the Society of Antiquaries of Scotland, 1960–61*

Morton, A.S., 'The Levellers of Galloway', in *Transactions of the Dumfriesshire & Galloway Natural History & Antiquarian Society*, Third Series, volume 19, 1936

Prevost, W.A.J., 'Letters Reporting the Rising of the Levellers in 1724', in *Transactions of the Dumfriesshire & Galloway Natural History & Antiquarian Society*, Third Series, volume 44, 1961

Smout, T.C., 'The Landowner and the Planned Village in Scotland, 1730–1830', in Phillipson, N. and Mitchison, R. (eds.), *Scotland in the Age of Improvement* (Edinburgh, 1963)

Whatley, Christopher, 'How Tame were the Scottish Lowlands during the eighteenth century?', in Devine, T. M. (ed.), *Conflict and Stability in Scottish Society, 1700–1850* (Edinburgh, 1990)

Books

Aitchison, Peter, *Children of the Sea: The Story of the Eyemouth Disaster* (East Linton, 2001)

Select Bibliography

Aiton, William, *General View of the Agriculture of the County of Ayr* (Glasgow, 1811)

Aiton, William, *General View of the Agriculture of the County of Bute* (Glasgow, 1816)

Ascherson, Neal, *Stone Voices: The Search for Scotland* (London: 2002)

Brown, Callum, *The Social History of Religion in Scotland since 1730* (London, 1987)

Campbell, R.H., *Scotland Since 1707: The Rise of an Industrial Society* (Oxford, 1965)

Craig, David, *On the Crofters' Trail* (London, 1990)

Craig, John, *Episodes of my life* (privately printed, 1928. Historical Collection of the Great Lakes, University of Bowling Green, Ohio, United States)

Cunningham, Ian C. (ed.), *The Nation Survey'd: Timothy Pont's Maps of Scotland* (East Linton, 2001)

Defoe, Daniel, *A Tour Through the Whole Island of Great Britain* (1962 edition)

Devine, T.M., *The Transformation of Rural Scotland* (Edinburgh, 1999)

Devine, T.M., *The Scottish Nation, 1700–2000* (London, 2001)

Devine, T. M. (ed.), *Conflict and Stability in Scottish Society, 1700–1850* (Edinburgh, 1990)

Devine, T.M. and Mitchison, Rosalind (eds.), *People and Society in Scotland, Volume 1, 1760–1830* (Edinburgh, 1988)

Dobson, David, *Directory of Scots Banished to the American Plantations, 1650–1775* (Baltimore, 1984)

Dobson, David, *Scottish Emigration to Colonial America, 1607–1785* (University of Georgia, 1988)

Drummond, A. and Bulloch, J., *The Scottish Church, 1688–1843: The Age of the Moderates* (Edinburgh 1973)

Fenton, Alexander, *Scottish Country Life* (East Linton, 1999)

Fenyö, Krisztina, *Contempt, Sympathy and Romance: Lowland Perceptions of the Highlands and the Clearances During the Famine Years, 1845–1855* (East Linton, 2000)

Fullerton, William, *General View of the Agriculture of the County of Ayr* (Edinburgh, 1793)

Fraser, David (ed.), *The Christian Watt Papers* (1988)

Galt, John, *Annals of the Parish* (Edinburgh edition, 1994)

Harper, Marjory, *Adventurers and Exiles* (London, 2003)

Hunter, James, *A Dance Called America* (Edinburgh, 1994)

Hunter, James, *The Making of the Crofting Community* (Edinburgh, 2000)

Logue, Kenneth, *Popular Disturbances in Scotland, 1780–1815* (Edinburgh, 1979)

Lowe, Alexander, *General View on the Agriculture of the County of Berwick* (London, 1794)

Lynch, Michael, *Scotland: A New History* (London, 1991)

Mackenzie, W.M., *The Book of Arran, Volume Second* (Brodick, Isle of Arran, 1982)
McCowan, D.B., *The McCowans of Scarborough* (Scarborough Historical Society, 1983)
McCowan, D.B., *Stockbriggs Estate, Scotland 1806–1831* (Toronto, 1992)
McCowan, D.B., *The McCowans of Cumnock, Lesmahagow and Scarborough* (Toronto, 1985)
McCowan, D.B., *Immigration from Lanarkshire and Dumfriesshire, 1797–1850* (Toronto, 1988)
McCowan, D.B., *To Sustene The Personis: The Agricultural Revolution* (Toronto, 1992)
McIlvanney, Liam, *Burns the Radical* (East Linton, 2002)
Mitchison, R., *A History of Scotland* (London, 1970)
Phillipson, N. and Mitchison, R. (eds.) *Scotland in the Age of Improvement* (Edinburgh, 1963)
Ramsay, J., *Scotland and Scotsmen in the eighteenth century* (Edinburgh and London, 1888)
Robertson, G., *Rural Recollections* (Irvine, 1820)
Saunders, L.J., *Scottish Democracy: The Social and Intellectual Background, 1815–1840* (Edinburgh, 1950)
Sinclair, Sir John (ed.), *The Statistical Account of Scotland, 1791–1797* (Edinburgh, 1791–7), 21 volumes. New edition ed. Grant, I. and Withrington, D. (Wakefield, 1975–1979)
Smout, T.C., *A History of the Scottish People, 1560–1830* (London, 1969)
Smout, T.C., *A Century of the Scottish People, 1830–1950* (London, 1986)
Somerville, A., *The Autobiography of a Working Man* (London, 1848)
Sprott, Gavin, *Robert Burns: Pride and Passion* (Edinburgh, 1996)
Stone, Jeffrey, *Illustrated Maps of Scotland* (London, 1991)
Strawhorn, John (ed.), *Ayrshire at the time of Burns* (Kilmarnock, 1959)
Whatley, Christopher, *Scottish Society, 1707–1830* (Manchester, 2000)
Yeoman, Louise, *Reportage Scotland* (Glasgow, 2000)

Index